KEEPING COOL ON THE CAMPAIGN TRAIL

101 OF "SILENT" CAL'S WISE INSIGHTS ON VOTING, CAMPAIGNING, AND GOVERNING

By Daniel L. Wrigl

KEEPING COOL ON THE CAMPAIGN TRAIL:

101 OF "SILENT" CAL'S WISE INSIGHTS ON
VOTING, CAMPAIGNING, AND GOVERNING

ISBN-13:

978-1511679787

ISBN-10:

1511679786

Cover Illustration by Daniel L. Wright

www.crackerpilgrim.com

To Mary and Midge

Acknowledgments

The process from idea to publication for this book has been four years in the making. It has been an effort to which many fine people have contributed and while any mistakes within these pages are solely the responsibility of the author, this work is infinitely better for those who helped bring it to completion.

First, I wish to thank Mr. Paul Carnahan, Librarian at the Vermont Historical Society in Barre. Without his dedicated efforts to hunt down answers to my inquiries, this book would not have happened. I am grateful for Mr. William Jenney, Site Administrator for the President Calvin Coolidge State Historic Site, whose work on my behalf is but a small part of the debt all Coolidge students owe him. I thank Silvia Mejia, Special Collections Librarian of the State Library of Massachusetts, for her generous assistance with the Coolidge Collection located in the archives there. I also greatly appreciate the help of Andrew Elder, Digital Archives and Outreach

Librarian, at the Joseph P. Healey Library in the University of Massachusetts. Amy McDonald, Assistant University Archivist of the David M. Rubenstein Rare Book and Manuscript Library at Duke University, also assisted kindly in locating elusive material on Coolidge and C. Bascom Slemp. I recognize the great research team at the Manuscript Division of the Library of Congress, namely Chamisa Redmond, for her meticulous care in answering questions and processing requests regarding the Everett Sanders and Edward T. Clark Papers. I also owe thanks to Anne Causey of the Albert and Shirley Small Special Collections Library at the University of Virginia for her assistance with the Slemp Papers. Without sound research, the recognition due Coolidge after ninety years would still be far out of reach.

The best research still requires solid guidance to make any work like this a success. To paraphrase Mr. Coolidge, I have perhaps been more fortunate than others for the good influences that have continued to come into life as a result of this project. I owe unremittable debts to Mr. Jerry Wallace and Mr. Jim Cooke, whose friendship, knowledge of Cal, and editorial expertise are invaluable to me and essential to what is written in these pages. Many thanks for the support of Mr. David Pietrusza, whose cogent analysis, patient direction, and scholarly input are always welcome. I am humbled and grateful for his contribution of a Preface to this work. Their enthusiasm and experienced counsel saved me from many a mistake and decisively improved this book. This offering is a labor of love born, in large measure, of their encouragement.

Most importantly, praise and recognition go to my wife, Mary, for her devotion and love. Her patient endurance of Mr. Coolidge, who has virtually been a continual guest in our home for four years, speaks to her grace, her worth, and her faith in things unseen. "What men owe to the love and help of good women can never be told."

Preface

"All in the Family" 's Archie Bunker was wont to croon "Mister, We Could Use a Man Like Herbert Hoover again."

Archie got it wrong, but chronologically not by that much. More and more people now realize we could certainly use a man like Calvin Coolidge again. It's not just a question of public policies. It is also a matter of character.

Character counts.

Without it, the best policies will never be implemented; the finest principles will never be articulated convincingly.

So that is something to watch in every election season—and what follows.

Daniel Wright, a powerful and persistent chronicler of the Coolidge record, has here endeavored to remind us of the Coolidge character and of Coolidge wisdom.

To some the Coolidge way may seem obvious. But if it is so obvious why have we strayed so far and so dangerously from it? It bears recollecting from as many sources as possible.

Daniel Wright has performed yet another admirable public service in reminding us of Mr. Coolidge. Hats off to him—and to Not-So-Silent Cal!

David Pietrusza

April 2015

Why Coolidge?

For many years the name Calvin Coolidge has been the butt of countless jokes, the subject of mockery and disdain, from intellectuals on down.[1] Portrayed by some as among the worst of Presidents, positioned inconspicuously between giants like Wilson and FDR, Coolidge is finally experiencing a reappraisal and renewed respect. It is forgotten how genuinely popular and esteemed this man was in his time, for very good reasons. Too many rush to condemn what they have been told about the man rather than learning of him firsthand, in his own words and on his own terms.

Yet, even those who have attempted to look beyond the layers of literary hostility to him still find Cal an enigma. This is because he so thoroughly defies the conventional path to political success. Never one to slap backs or schmooze, Cal not only proved he could win election after election but he could widen his margins each time and convince Democrats and the unaffiliated to join the team long

---

[1] Thomas B. Silver, Coolidge and the Historians (Durham: Carolina Academic, 1982) 7-8.

before Reagan demonstrated it could be done.

Stringing together an impressive twenty-one victories from city council to President of the United States, Coolidge came to the White House with more practical political experience than most of our Chief Executives. He rose not by constantly redefining who he was or what he believed but by quietly proving worthy of ever greater responsibility in faithfulness to his oath and to the day's work. Amassing an extraordinary record of accomplishments, Cal did while others merely promised to do.

The only President born on the Fourth of July, he had the highest regard for the Declaration and America's founding principles. However, he was no reactionary or weakling, strengthening the Office of the Presidency, preserving six years of peace at home, and deftly handling public relations, while encouraging the development of radio, aviation, and other modern innovations. He showed that true progress retains roots in the Founding, not in spite of it. A lifelong advocate of our party system, he was no mindless follower but did his own thinking, rejected the conventional, and proved it could succeed. His reserve was not indecision or weakness but by shrewdly downplaying his ability to get things done, he cut through all the usual talk, good intentions, and lack of results that usually accompany the empty fanfare of most politicians. Confident in his abilities, and having sought all the information he could, Coolidge always made his own decisions.

Perhaps this paradoxical quality of "Silent" Cal is why it has become easier to lampoon the man and his era than to understand him. He certainly left us a vast body of work from which to judge his record: 521 press conferences (an average 7.8 conferences per month, a quantity no subsequent President has matched, not even FDR in four terms), a 4,055-word Inaugural Address, six 6,000-word Annual Messages, some twenty annual speeches of 3,000 words each, totaling an average 75,000 words per year for six years.[2] He was anything but "silent" as Coolidge just

---

[2] Calvin Coolidge, The Autobiography (New York: Cosmopolitan, 1929) 221.

as scholar Jerry L. Wallace reveals, stating that a full 30% of his Presidential speeches were delivered through the new technology.[3]

Perhaps the reason then, for his mischaracterization comes not so much for its resemblance to truth as for his inexplicable authenticity and actual effectiveness. It was hardly an idle boast when Coolidge confidently asserted after six years that most of his more than five dozen proposals, made at the start of his administration, had become law by 1929.[4]

He achieved what no other President has since, a $1 billion budget surplus every year he was in office, taxes reduced four times, and a $9.8 billion reduction in the National Debt during the Harding and Coolidge years, paying down an average $120 million in annual interest. Not even Ronald Reagan, who studiously admired Coolidge, came close to that level of success.

---

[3] Jerry L. Wallace, Calvin Coolidge: Our First Radio President (Plymouth Notch: Calvin Coolidge Memorial Foundation, 2008) 1.

[4] Coolidge, The Autobiography 225.

Had these actions been the only legacy secured by Cal, he would have been impressive enough, yet he did more. He restored faith in the people's government by cleaning up the corruption occurring during the administration of his predecessor, punishing those who broke the law and refusing to condemn the innocent.

He reaffirmed equality and due process under the law after years of arbitrary civil rights abuses under the Wilson administration, pardoning dozens unjustly targeted under the Espionage Act. While others engaged in race-baiting or campaigns planted in bigotry, he spoke firmly against racial and religious intolerance. He worked to undo segregation in the Executive Branch, tried to create both a Federal anti-lynching law and a commission to heal race relations, defended groups targeted by the KKK, and treated people on the basis of merit instead of color or creed.

He was the first to recognize Native Americans as full citizens in 1924 and fought for their assimilation freed of Government paternalism.

He twice vetoed the government takeover of agriculture and advocated personal initiative and cooperation as the answer, not centralized price fixing and market manipulation.

He signed the Immigration Act of 1924, rebuking its prejudices while understanding that anything but slow assimilation into American citizenship would overwhelm the system and destroy opportunity for everyone, both those already here and those who would arrive to become Americans in the future.

He was the first President to make full use of the medium of radio, encouraging its establishment as an innovative and useful form of communication nationwide. He promoted the advancement of air travel and aeronautical possibilities.

His consistent efforts to actually reduce government spending, return the annual surpluses to taxpayers, and scale back the size and reach of government in deference to personal, local, and state governance laid the foundation for one of the strongest economic booms this country has ever seen. It was a growth that was both broad and deep, bringing ownership and opportunity to millions who, for the first time, were able to work a five day work week and yet afford leisure and recreation, travel by automobile, and a growing list of household conveniences.

Lynching and mortality rates went down as disease prevention improved and prosperity reached into the homes of minorities, all without the need for expansive legislation.

Business and labor thrived not through government preferences but through increased freedom and competition.

Peace was maintained through a policy of disinterested fairness to all coupled with sufficient strength to defend our citizens and their property, first and foremost. Each country would be expected to govern itself but know that America stood by to help, not to exploit. Those who defied the law would find the United States ready to hold the violent and disobedient accountable for their actions.

In Coolidge, the nation knew it had calm, confidence, and courage to lead, not through coercive saber-rattling or Federal sanctions done for effect, but through just dealing and a mature commitment to restoring constitutional government, meeting our obligations at home and abroad.

For Coolidge, however, politics had to consist of something more than theoretical abstractions; it had to remain practical, ever-close to realities, in order to serve people. The people were to be master of their own government not subservient to it.

This is a book for voters, candidates, and officeholders. It brings together a sampling of the insights, experiences, and principles of one of America's wisest Presidents and most successful statesmen. Coolidge's long career from local party leadership to the Presidency equips him with a unique credibility to help forge sounder government that starts with good citizenship. Government improves not by an edict from the top but with good citizenship from the individual. When each one becomes a better citizen, a better candidate, and a public servant worthy of public trust, then (and only then) will government start to improve, Coolidge taught.

This book is more concerned with how to uphold our obligations as free men and women in this constitutional Republic than merely how to win one particular race or election cycle. This book gives us a glimpse into how Coolidge rose to America's highest office, how he won honorably, and served faithfully. He has much to teach us if we are ready to receive it.

1. Action

"Though he is essentially a man of action, he has always said very little about what he was doing. To the last possible degree, he lets the act tell the story."[5]

2. Appointments

"What we need in appointive positions is [sic] men of knowledge and experience who have sufficient character to resist temptations. If that standard is maintained, we need not be concerned about their former activities...The public service would be improved if all vacancies were filled by simply appointing the best ability and character that can be found."[6]

After striving to select the most competent person, as Fuess summarizes, Coolidge "left them to do their jobs in their own way, without petty interference, giving them complete authority and unqualified support. He was seldom inquisitive or fussy or jealous

---

[5] Robert A. Woods, The Preparation of Calvin Coolidge (Cambridge: Riverside, 1924) 206.

[6] Coolidge, The Autobiography 227-228.

or dictatorial. His appointees felt that they could, in emergencies, use their own judgment and be sure that he would not desert them. The final decision in major problems had to be his, but he was usually guided by the advice of those whom he had picked. They, in turn, appreciating their freedom and confidence, had their loyalty strengthened."[7]

When it came to appointing judges, Coolidge's central question was, "If I appoint him a judge, can he see the issues of the case over the heads of the parties? I do not intend to appoint any man to the Superior Court, or to any court, who cannot do that."[8]

3. Authenticity

"My grandfather Coolidge wore a blue woolen frock much of the time, which is a most convenient garment for that

---

[7] Claude M. Fuess, Calvin Coolidge: The Man From Vermont (Boston: Little, Brown, and Company, 1940) 406-407.

[8] Fuess 482. Fuess goes on to say, "Coolidge's appointments were sometimes criticized, but he always gave them careful study."

region...When I went to visit the old home in later years I liked to wear the one he left, with some fine calf-skin boots about two sizes too large for me, which were made for him when he went to the Vermont legislature about 1858. When news pictures began to be taken of me there, I found that among the public this was generally supposed to be a makeup costume, which it was not, so I have since been obliged to forego the comfort of wearing it. In public life it is sometimes necessary in order to appear really natural to be actually artificial."[9]

4. Bureaucracy

"No method of procedure has ever been devised by which liberty could be divorced from local self-government. No plan of centralization has ever been adopted which did not result in bureaucracy, tyranny, inflexibility, reaction, and decline. Of all forms of government, those administered by bureaus are about the least satisfactory to an enlightened and progressive people. Being irresponsible they become autocratic, and

[9] Coolidge, The Autobiography 22.

being autocratic they resist all development. Unless bureaucracy is constantly resisted it breaks down representative government and overwhelms democracy. It is the one element in our institutions that sets up the pretense of having authority over everybody and being responsible to nobody."[10]

5. Business of America

"When I have been referring to business, I have used the word in its all-inclusive sense to denote alike the employer and employee, the production of agriculture and industry, the distribution of transportation and commerce, and the service of finance and banking. It is the work of the world...

"In its great economic organization it does not represent, as some have hastily concluded, a mere desire to minister to selfishness...It is something far more important than a sordid desire for gain. It

---

[10] Calvin Coolidge, Foundations of the Republic: Speeches and Addresses (New York: Charles Scribner's Sons, 1926) 410-411. This is an excerpt from address given at College of William and Mary, May 15, 1926.

could not successively succeed on that basis...it rests on a higher law. True business represents the mutual organized effort of society to minister to the economic requirements of civilization. It is an effort by which men provide for the material needs of each other. While it is not an end in itself, it is the important means for the attainment of the supreme end. It rests squarely on the law of service. It has for its main reliance truth and faith and justice. In its larger sense it is one of the greatest contributing forces to the moral and spiritual advancement of the race."[11]

6. Campaigns

"A political campaign can be justified only on the grounds that it enables the citizens to become informed as to what policies are best for themselves and for their country, in order that they may vote to elect those who from their past record and present professions they know will put such policies into effect. The purpose of a campaign is to send an

---

[11] Ibid, 319-320. Coolidge was addressing the New York Chamber of Commerce, November 19, 1925.

intelligent and informed voter to the ballot box. All the speeches, all the literature, all the organization, all the effort, all the time and all the money, which are not finally registered on election day, are wasted."[12]

7. Candidates

"For important political service the three qualifications necessary are character, ability and experience. Some of our voters are not giving sufficient consideration to these requirements. They are often supporting candidates whose greatest appeal is that they are good fellows. An agreeable personality is a fine quality, but it is not enough to administer a great office. It is vain to support office seekers who smile, if it results in electing officeholders who are not competent. The government cannot be run successfully by substituting the power of entertainment for the power of accomplishment."[13]

---

[12] Ibid, 176-177. This is taken from a radio address delivered from the White House, November 3, 1924.
[13] Edward C. Lathem, ed, Calvin Coolidge Says: Over three hundred dispatches prepared by former-

"The beginning of good government is in good nominations. It is time we gave serious and conscientious attention to our right to vote by nominating the best qualified candidates...Unless we make our nominations on merit, public questions will not be decided on merit."[14]

"We have in this country a certain type of officeholder, fortunately not large, who are always out with square and compass seeking to find out what the political effect will be of every action they take...Any one with a little experience can tell them in advance that the effect of an action based on such motives will always be bad. All the predominant political opinion of the nation which is worth cultivating is never impressed by decisions made for effect. Those who compose that body want responsible officeholders to try to find out what is best for the welfare of the

---

President Coolidge and syndicated to newspapers in the United States and abroad during 1930-1931 (Plymouth: Calvin Coolidge Memorial Foundation, 1972) 155; Excerpt from daily column dated October 8, 1930.

[14] Ibid 109; Column from August 15, 1930.

people and do that. They are moved by sincerity and integrity of purpose. Pretense does not appeal to them. That is the reason why those who seek popularity so seldom find it, while those who follow an informed conscience so often are astonished by a wide public approval. The people know a sham even when they seem to be trying to fool themselves and they cannot help having a wholesome respect for a reality. The best political effect usually comes to those who disregard it."[15]

8. Character

"That which we call character in all men is not a matter of hire and salary...Those in whom is placed the solemn duty of caring for others ought to think of themselves last or their decisions will lack authority. There is apparent a disposition to deny the disinterestedness and impartiality of government. Such charges are the result of ignorance and an evil desire to destroy our institutions for personal profit. It is of infinite importance to demonstrate that

---

[15] Ibid 161; October 15, 1930.

legislation is used not for the benefit of the legislator, but of the public."[16]

"Character is the only secure foundation of the State. We know well that all plans of improving the machinery of government and all measures for social betterment fail, and the hopes of progress wither, when corruption touches administration...I am a Republican but I can not on that account shield anyone because he is a Republican. I am a Republican, but I can not on that account prosecute anyone because he is a Democrat. I want no hue and cry, no mingling of innocent and guilty in unthinking condemnation, no confusion of mere questions of law with questions of fraud and corruption...I ask the support of our people, as chief magistrate, intent on the enforcement of our laws without fear or favor, no matter who is hurt or what the consequences."[17]

---

[16] Coolidge, Have Faith in Massachusetts: A Collection of Speeches and Messages (Boston: Houghton Mifflin, 1919) 173, 174-175. Excerpt from then-Governor Coolidge's veto of a salary increase measure passed by the state legislature in 1919.
[17] Richardson, James D., ed, Supplement to the

"If our republic is to be maintained and improved it will be through the efforts and character of the individual. It will be, first of all, because of the influences which exist in the home, for it is the ideals which prevail in the home life which make up the strength of the nation."[18]

9. Citizenship

"We must aim to impress upon each citizen the individual duty to be a sincere student of public problems, in order that he may rightly render the service which his citizenship exacts."[19]

Messages and Papers of the Presidents (New York: Bureau of National Literature, 1929) 9378-9379. This was part of an address Coolidge gave to the National Republican Club in New York City, February 12, 1924.

[18] Coolidge, The Price of Freedom: Speeches and Addresses (New York: Charles Scribner's Sons, 1924) 346; Part of the Memorial Day Address given by Vice President Coolidge in Northampton, Massachusetts, May 30, 1923.
[19] A selection from address given by President Coolidge before the Thirty-Third Continental Congress of the Daughters of the American Revolution, April 14, 1924.

"Your country wants not only your votes but your influence in all coming elections. By this I do not mean to appeal in behalf of any party. I appeal in behalf of our common country."[20]

10. Civil Rights

"Our Constitution guarantees equal rights to all our citizens, without discrimination on account of race or colour. I have taken my oath to support the Constitution. It is the source of your rights and my rights. I propose to regard it, and administer it, as the source of the rights of all the people, whatever their belief or race. A coloured man is precisely as much entitled to submit his candidacy in a party primary as is any other citizen. The decision must be made by the constituents to whom he offers himself, and by nobody else. You have suggested that in some fashion I should bring influence to bear to prevent the possibility of a coloured man being nominated for Congress. In reply,

---

[20] Also taken from the address before the Daughters of the American Revolution, Washington, D. C., April 14, 1924.

I quote my great predecessor, Theodore Roosevelt: 'I cannot consent to take the position that the door of hope—the door of opportunity—is to be shut upon any man, no matter how worthy, purely upon the grounds of race or colour.' "[21]

"Our country has many elements in its population, many different modes of thinking and living, all of which are striving in their own way to be loyal to the high ideals worthy of the crown of American citizenship. It is fundamental of our institutions that they seek to guarantee to all our inhabitants the right to live their own lives under the protection of the public law. This does not include any license to injure others materially, physically, morally, to incite revolution, or to violate the established customs which have long had the sanction of enlightened society. But it does mean the full right to liberty and equality before the law without distinction of race

[21] C. Bascom Slemp, ed. The Mind of the President: As Revealed by Himself in His Own Words (Garden City, NY: Doubleday, Page & Company, 1926) 248; Excerpt of a letter from President Coolidge to Sgt. Charles F. Gardner of New York, August 9, 1924.

and creed. This condition can not be granted to others, or enjoyed by ourselves, except by the application of the principle of broadest tolerance. Bigotry is only another name for slavery. It reduces to serfdom not only those against whom it is directed, but also those who seek to apply it. An enlarged freedom can only be secured by the application of the golden rule."[22]

11. Civility and Confrontation

Much has been made of the need for a higher tone of civility in politics, appealing to the example of Coolidge as precedent for it. To Coolidge, civility did not mean passive tolerance or avoidance of political contrast. It is consequently overlooked how unapologetically partisan Coolidge could be at times. There was a proper place for party opposition and partisanship:

"The American people are turning from the contemplation of a mirage which, for a time, they mistook for a reality. When the political history of the past eight years is written it

[22] Richardson 9537; Third Annual Message, December 8, 1925.

will resemble nothing so much a chapter of accidents...The charge laid against Republicans of countenancing the wicked principle of putting the dollar above the man, was entirely outdone by the Democratic practice, which put the dollar completely out of reach of the man...The very spirit of America withered, and the glory of the nation for the time departed...

"The Republican Party has not been, is not lacking in idealism either in its history, purposes or leaders. Who can name an established ideal they have not cherished? There is none. It has now furnished four-fifths of the States necessary to enroll the idealism of the Nation through equal suffrage...In support of these candidates and the principles they represent, the country is turning again to realities. It wants to turn away from the mirage of false hopes and false security. It wants to be done with miasma of war. It was the security of peace. It wants to live again under the government of the Constitution."[23]

---

[23] David Pietrusza, ed., Calvin Coolidge: A Documentary Biography (Church & Reid Books, 2013) 119, 120, 124; Address on September 18,

It was during Coolidge's first term as president of the Massachusetts Senate that he clashed with Governor David Walsh, a Democrat, over a particular bill awaiting the governor's signature. Heading over to the governor's office, Coolidge discovered that the bill had not yet been signed. The governor's secretary then instructed, "Come around tomorrow, senator, and I will give you the pen which he uses in its veto." Just as quickly, Senator Coolidge shot back, "No, Mr. Secretary, I won't take it as a gift, but I will swap it for the pen which I use to sign the bill passed over his veto." With that, Coolidge turned and walked out. Governor Walsh knew that, with Coolidge, an override was no empty boast. The bill was signed.[24]

Coolidge understood that there was a wide berth for disagreement. Intense partisan dissent did not spell the end of our Republic and should not be treated with anxiety and

---

1920, before the Republican Nominating Convention which named as candidate for Governor of Massachusetts, the man who would succeed Coolidge in 1921.

[24] Roland D. Sawyer, Cal Coolidge, President (Boston: Four Seas Company, 1924) 98-99.

trepidation, as if it did. Instead, Coolidge sought to exemplify the cool-headed judgment and sense of perspective with which he approached all public issues. He demonstrated an example for others to follow if they wish but partisanship was not itself the enemy, as this occasion from the summer of 1921 illustrates. When two of the most irascible partisans, Democrat James Reed and Republican Porter McCumber, of the decade began trading accusations on the Senate floor, the rhetoric escalated with "liar" and demands to "step outside" while calls to intervene were urgently made to the Chair. Turning toward Vice President Coolidge, the presiding officer of the Senate who sat quietly at the front of the room, Senators and visitors alike expected the gavel to bang and demands for order to be issued. Instead, Cal calmly replied, "I shall, if they get excited."[25]

Civility, for Coolidge, did not preclude his firm resolve to confront others, forcing those

---

[25] William Allen White, Calvin Coolidge: The Man Who Is President (New York: Macmillan Company, 1925) 116.

of both parties to explain their positions to voters. When Coolidge faced opposition, the solution was not to surrender the field to appear open-minded or magnanimous but rather to demonstrate the strength of his position with logic, confidence and a strong measure of wit. He never arrived at a position hastily considered. As such, he expected those around him to exercise the same thorough certainty.

He cared nothing for electoral costs from the positions he took. He took them because, having thought them through, knew they were right. If he lost, he could return home, preserving integrity whatever the result might be. As Woods notes, "He never precipitates controversy, but will always take a firm stand. Fighting in never his choice; but when a conflict is forced upon him, he goes into it, and through it to the end, with decision and precision."[26]

He was not a man to see "moral victory" in Republican losses either. The belief in our system, limited government, low taxes and freedom under law deserved full support, no

---

[26] Woods 32.

less by those who wear the name, "Republican." The name stood for specific principles. The name entailed worthy ideas to be defended and explained not discarded and apologized for every election cycle. It was never a virtuous or wise thing to teach others a lesson by deliberately withholding support for these principles or the candidates who espoused them in order to protect a convoluted, purist view of Party pecking order. Coolidge knew that a courageous and truthful articulation of sound principles deserves and keeps the public trust. Anything short of empowering informed voters with a full realization of the policies and leadership they are going to get in their candidate, the campaign is a failure. To cater to, as individuals or as political parties, the disingenuous, fraudulent or pandering politician is not civility; it is a repudiation of sound government and a betrayal of faithful service to the people.

"Last night at Somerville I spoke on some of the fundamental differences between the Republican and Democratic policies, and showed how we were dependent on Republican principles as a foundation on

35

which to erect any advance in our social and economic welfare. This year the Republican Party has adopted a very advanced platform. That was natural, for we have always been the party of progress, and have given our attention to that, when we were not engaged in a life-and-death struggle to overcome the fallacies put forth by our opponents, with which we are all so familiar."[27]

"In this time of stress, we need strong, party organization and we do not have them. Of course, almost every democrat thinks the sovereign remedy for any of our ills is an appropriation of public money. A good many republicans always think so too."[28]

"For more than two generations the Republican Party has been one of the most effective instruments of popular government that ever existed...When the country has had a great task to perform it has instinctively turned to the Republican Party...It is a time

---

[27] Coolidge, Have Faith in Massachusetts 51; From a speech he gave to the Norfolk Republican Club in Boston, October 9, 1916.

[28] Calvin Coolidge, letter to Edward T. Clark, 28 May 1932, Edward T. Clark Papers, Manuscript Division, Library of Congress, Washington, D. C.

when the great body of our people of common sense should not be stampeded, but should stand firm. In spite of all declarations to the contrary, of the professions of platforms and candidates, the record of two generations discloses that the safety of the country lies in the success of the principles of the Republican Party."[29]

12. Confidence in America's People

"Faith in the American people means a faith in their ability to form sound judgments, when once the facts have been presented to them clearly and without prejudice."[30]

"Our most sacred trust has been, and is, the establishment and expansion of the spirit of democracy. No doubt we shall take some false starts and experience some disappointing reactions. But we have put our confidence in the ultimate wisdom of the people. We believe we can rely on their

[29] Calvin Coolidge, "The Republican Case," Saturday Evening Post 10 September 1932: 3, 72.
[30] Richardson 9393; From a speech given by Coolidge at the Annual Luncheon of the Associated Press, New York City, April 22, 1924.

intelligence, their honesty, and their character. We are thoroughly committed to the principle that they are better fitted to govern themselves than anyone else is to govern them. We do not claim immediate perfection. But we do expect continual progress. Our history reveals that in such expectation we have not been disappointed. It is better for the people to make their own mistakes than to have some one else make their mistakes for them."[31]

13. Constitution and Law

"I am opposed to the practice of a legislative deception. It is better to proceed with candor...My oath was not to take a chance on the Constitution. It was to support it. When the proponents of this measure do not intend to jeopardize their safety by acting under it, why should I jeopardize my oath by approving it? We have had too much legislating by clamor, by tumult, by pressure. Representative government ceases when

---

[31] Ibid 9755-9756; Portion of his Address before the Sixth Pan-American Conference, Havana, Cuba, January 16, 1928.

outside influence of any kind is substituted for the judgment of the representative. This does not mean that the opinion of constituents is to be ignored. It is to be weighed most carefully, for the representative must represent, but his oath provides that it must be 'faithfully and impartially to the best of his abilities and understanding, agreeably to the rules and regulations of the Constitution and laws.' Opinions and instructions do not outmatch the Constitution. Against it they are void...There can be no constitutional instruction to do an unconstitutional act."[32]

"What is the law? Well, follow it."

This was President Coolidge's signature way of resolving questions placed before him, as then-Attorney General John G. Sargent recounts. This obvious yet all too overlooked approach to resolving issues is reaffirmed in Coolidge's Autobiography, "All situations that arise are likely to be simplified, and

---

[32] Pietrusza, <u>A Documentary Biography</u> 98-99; Excerpt from Governor Coolidge's veto of Bill to Regulate Manufacture and Sale of Beer, Cider, and Light Wines, issued May 6, 1920.

many of them completely solved, by an application of the Constitution and the law. If what they require to be done, is done, there is no opportunity for criticism, and it would be seldom that anything better could be devised...So their problem was solved like many others by simply finding out what the law required."[33]

14. Contributions

"My campaign was carried on in careful compliance with the law, and the expense was within the allowed limit of $1,500, which was contributed by numerous people. I was thus under no special obligation to any one for raising money for me."[34]

"I do not like as a matter of principle large contributions given to campaign funds, because they create a bad impression and give the idea of a wrongful motive. But I think that it would be well to keep in mind that it isn't so much the size of the contribution as the purpose for which it is

---

[33] John G. Sargent, "Championing the Negro," Good Housekeeping June 1935: 201-202.
[34] Coolidge, Autobiography 114-115.

given. I can imagine a very large contribution that would be given for a perfectly justifiable purpose, and I can imagine a very small contribution that might be made for an entirely unjustifiable purpose."[35]

15. Courage

When a municipal ordinance prohibiting jitneys began to be disregarded, it came to the attention of Governor Coolidge, who instructed the railroad trustees to replace the illegal jitneys with street cars, as the law stipulated.

" 'If you do that,' said a man, 'the labor people will go into every town of the State and crucify you politically'...The Governor patiently listened for a while, and then broke in, with a drawl that convulsed the listeners and embarrassed the speaker, saying: 'Don't let me deter you. Go right ahead.' At the same hearing, after the conference had dragged on, one of the committee remarked: 'well, about all we have done so far is to pass

---

[35] Slemp, Mind of the President 89; Coolidge spoke these words during a press conference, April 11, 1924.

the buck.' The Governor looked right at the speaker and said: 'Try it on me. I won't pass the buck.' "[36]

"There is no right to strike against the public safety by anybody, anywhere, anytime."

"His friends, aghast, urged him not to send such a telegram. They said it meant the end of his political career.

'Very likely,' said Governor Coolidge—and sent the telegram."[37]

16. Criticism

"Public men must expect criticism and be prepared to endure false charges from their opponents. It is a matter of no great concern to them. But public confidence in government is a matter of great concern...It is necessary to differentiate between partisan assertions and actual conditions." This is

[36] M. E. Hennessey, Calvin Coolidge: From a Green Mountain Farm to the White House (New York: G. P. Putnam's Sons, 1924) 112-113.

[37] McKee, John Hiram. Coolidge Wit and Wisdom: 125 Short Stories About "Cal" (New York: Frederick A. Stokes, 1933) 27.

how Coolidge could assert with all honesty, "I have often said that there was no cause for feeling disturbed at being misrepresented in the press. It would be only when they began to say things detrimental to me which were true that I should feel alarm. Perhaps one of the reasons I have been a target for so little abuse is because I have tried to refrain from abusing other people."[38]

For Coolidge criticism was not something to be avoided at all costs, as is the case with some politicians. In fact, it could be a sign that one was effective and should remain on course, as he once encouraged Treasury Secretary Andrew Mellon:

"Don't let what Senator ----- said about you in the Senate today bother you. I consider an attack from such a source a commendation."[39]

Coolidge once told an astonished officeholder, "If you can not stand criticism, you had better get out of public life."[40]

---

[38] Coolidge, Have Faith in Massachusetts 41; Autobiography 185-186.
[39] Andrew W. Mellon, "When Blame Was Praise," Good Housekeeping February 1935: 181.
[40] Joel T. Boone, "The Wrong 'Aye, Aye,' " Good

17. Declaring Candidacy

"It is much better not to press a candidacy too much, but to let it develop on its own merits without artificial stimulation. If the people want a man they will nominate him, if they do not want him he had best let the nomination go to another."[41]

18. Delegation

Coolidge understood the importance of delegation. Had the President assumed each Department's responsibilities, it would have questioned the faith which the people place in their government.

Ted Clark, handing the President Labor Department papers for review: 'Secretary Davis wants to know what you think.'

Coolidge: 'You tell ol' man Davis, I hired him as Secretary of Labor and if he can't do the job I'll get a new Secretary of Labor.' "[42]

Housekeeping April 1935: 40.

[41] Coolidge, Autobiography 120-121.

[42] Edmund Starling, Starling of the White House (Chicago: People's Book Club, 1916) 209.

"It is not sufficient to entrust details to some one else. They must be entrusted to some one who is competent."[43]

19. Deliberation

"We have had too much legislating by clamor, by tumult, by pressure. Representative government ceases when outside influence of any kind is substituted for the judgment of the representative. This does not mean that the opinion of constituents is to be ignored. It is to be weighed most carefully, for the representative must represent, but his oath provides that it must be 'faithfully and impartially according to the best of his abilities and understanding, agreeably to the rules and regulations of the Constitution and laws.' "[44]

---

[43] Coolidge, Autobiography 198.

[44] Pietrusza, Documentary Biography 99; Veto Message by Governor Coolidge, May 6, 1920.

20. Dogs

"Any man who does not like dogs and want them about does not deserve to be in the White House."[45]

Friend and political lieutenant during the 1924 campaign, William M. Butler says, "I think he enjoyed most of all [about the White House] the pets he felt free at last to have—the dogs, the cats, the guinea pigs, the birds, and last but not least, the pet raccoon, Rebecca...He delighted to give his dogs tidbits from the table, and I can hear his laconic voice exclaim 'Pie!' and see the rush of those two delightful white collies, Rob Roy and Prudence Prim, to his side in the great dining room."[46]

[45] Carl Sferrazza Anthony, <u>America's First Families: An Inside View of 200 Years of Private Life in the White House</u> (New York: Touchstone Book, 2001) 241.

[46] William M. Butler, "Uncle Sam's Front Porch," <u>Good Housekeeping</u> May 1935: 258.

21. Duty

"The conduct of public affairs is not a game. Responsible office does not go to the crafty. Governments are not founded upon an association for public plunder, but on the co-operation of men wherein each is seeking to do his duty."[47]

22. Economics

"Isn't it a strange thing that in every period of social unrest, men have the notion that they can pass a law and suspend the operations of economic law?"[48]

"It is not possible to repeal the law of supply and demand, of cause and effect, or of action and reaction. Value is a matter of opinion. An act of Congress has small jurisdiction over what men think."[49]

[47] Coolidge, Have Faith in Massachusetts 263-264; Taken from a speech given at Tremont Temple, November 1, 1919.
[48] Bruce Barton, "A President Shouldn't Know Too Much," Good Housekeeping March 1935: 221.
[49] Lathem, Calvin Coolidge Says 94; Column from July 29, 1930.

23. Electability

A discussion involving close friend and college classmate Dwight Morrow once broke out over whether Coolidge was electable as President. Most disagreed that he would ever make it, having neither the usual political gravitas or outgoing personality, besides,

" 'No one would like him!'

It was then that Morrow's daughter, Anne, spoke up:

'I like Mr. Coolidge. He was the only one who asked about my sore finger!'

To which her father rebutted the skeptics, 'There's your answer.' "[50]

"Even as a fledgling statesman, he knew how to keep party workers cheerful and enthusiastic and seldom neglected to give the chairman of each Republican town committee a word of commendation. He remembered all the little personal details

---

[50] Mrs. Dwight W. Morrow, "A Little Girl's Sore Finger," Good Housekeeping February 1935:185.

which count so much. An extraordinary number of extant letters, all brief, give evidence of his essential humanity, of his interest in birth and marriage and death, in all that people say and do."[51]

24. Expertise

"I made progress because I studied subjects sufficiently to know a little more about them than any one else on the floor."[52]

"The professionals in Boston soon discovered that they could teach him very little regarding politics as a fine art. He had a sleuth's instinct for learning what was going on, and he knew how to keep his fences mended." Judge Field once commented about his former law clerk, Coolidge's "greatness did not lie in his contacts with men. But as a politician he was brilliant. He seemed to know what people were thinking and how they would act."[53]

---

[51] Fuess 481.

[52] Coolidge, Autobiography 103.

[53] Fuess 481.

"What I have ever been able to do has been the result of first learning how to do it. I am not gifted with intuition. I need not only hard work but experience to be ready to solve problems. The presidents who have gone to Washington without first having held some national office have been at great disadvantage. It takes them a long time to become acquainted with the Federal officeholders and the Federal Government. Meanwhile they have had difficulty in dealing with the situation."[54]

25. Exporting Democracy

"Ultimately nations, like individuals, cannot depend upon each other but must depend upon themselves. Each one must work out its own salvation. We have every desire to help. But with all our resources we are powerless to save unless our efforts meet with a constructive response. The situation in our own country and all over the world is one that can be improved only by hard work and self-denial."[55]

---

[54] Ibid 145.
[55] Richardson 9466; Coolidge's Second Annual

"America stands ready to bear its share of the burdens of the world, but it cannot live the life of other peoples, it cannot remove from them the necessity of working out their own destiny. It recognizes their independence and the right to establish their own form of government, but America will join no nation in destroying what it believes ought to be preserved or in profaning what it believes ought to be held sacred."[56]

26. Expressing the Popular Will

"I felt at the time that the speeches I made and the statements I issued had a clearness of thought and revealed a power I had not before been able to express, which confirmed my belief that, when a duty comes to us, with it a power comes to enable us to perform it."[57]

Message read before Congress, December 3, 1924.
[56] Coolidge, The Price of Freedom: Speeches and Addresses (New York: Charles Scribner's Sons, 1924) 148; Speech before Johns Hopkins University, Baltimore, Maryland, February 22, 1922.
[57] Coolidge, Autobiography 133.

"Under a government such as ours and the method provided for the selection of the President, the man who occupies that office, in his temperament, attitudes, and characteristics, will well represent generally the inarticulate opinion of the public as to the kind of leadership the country needs at the time...Coolidge personified to our people calmness, high character, common sense with purpose, and splendid courage. The popularity of Coolidge, notwithstanding the opposition he encountered from a Congress nominally Republican, was due to the fact that he, not it, best understood the people, and they him."[58]

27. Equality

"With it [freedom] went the principle of equality, not an equality of possessions, not an equality of degree, but an equality in the attributes of humanity, an equality of kind. Each is possessed of the divine power to know the truth. It is in accordance with these standards that the American people

---

[58] Charles G. Dawes, "He Saw Beyond Congress," Good Housekeeping March 1935: 224.

adopted their Constitution and set up their government...If freedom and equality are not to be maintained, then there must be servitude and class distinction. If all the people are not to be permitted to rule, then there must be a rule of a part of the people. If there is not to be self-government, there must be some form of despotic government. If the individual is not to have the dollar which he himself earns, then he must be forced to hand it over to some one who has not earned it. Those who advocate a change in our standards, a change in our ideals, a change in our institutions, a change in our theory of government, can only proceed in this direction. No other course is open to them."[59]

28. Fairness

Serving as Physician to the President, Dr. James F. Coupal says of Coolidge, "It was a pleasure to watch the President's mind at work. It was like a slide rule—and just as

---

[59] Coolidge, Price of Freedom 233-234; Address given to Evanston Sunday Afternoon Club, Evanston, Illinois, January 21, 1923.

accurate. He hated unfairness, and his sense of justice made him think he was perfectly appointed by God." Lest someone misunderstand that last statement, Dr. Coupal explains, "If you had a mean thought about your rival, Calvin Coolidge would want to make you suffer for it."[60]

29. Foreign Relations

"On what nations are at home depends what they will be abroad. If the spirit of freedom rules in their domestic affairs, it will rule in their foreign affairs...We increase the desire for peace everywhere by being peaceful. We maintain a military force for our defence, but our offensive lies in the justice of our cause...We seek concord with all nations through mutual understanding. We believe in treaties and covenants and international law as a permanent record for a reliable determination of action. All these are evidences of a right intention. But something more than these is required, to maintain the peace of the world. In its final determination,

---

[60] James F. Coupal, "Football 'Medicine,' " <u>Good Housekeeping</u> March 1935: 220.

it must come from the heart of the people. Unless it abides there, we cannot build for it any artificial lodging place...Governments can do much for the betterment of the world. They are the instruments through which humanity acts in international relations. Because they cannot do everything, they must not neglect to do what they can. But the final establishment of peace, the complete maintenance of good will toward men, will be found only in the righteousness of the people of the earth."[61]

30. Form of Government Makes/Breaks Peace

"Next to our attachment to the principle of self-government has been our attachment to the policy of peace...Nowhere among these republics have great military establishments ever been maintained for the purpose of overawing or subjugating other nations...But it is one thing to be prepared to defend our rights as a last extremity and quite another to rely on force where reason ought to

[61] Slemp, Mind of the President 26; Portion of address Coolidge gave at the Annual Luncheon of the Associated Press, New York City, April 22, 1924.

prevail. The form of our governments guarantees us against the Old World dynastic wars. It is scarcely too much to say that the conflicts which have been waged by our republics for one hundred and fifty years have been almost entirely for the purpose of securing independence and extending the domain of human freedom. When these have been accomplished, we have not failed to heed the admonition to beat our swords into plowshares.

"We have kept the peace so largely among our republics because democracies are peace-moving. They are founded on the desire to promote the general welfare of the people, which is seldom accomplished by warfare."[62]

31. Freedom

"I want the people of American to be able to work less for the Government and more for themselves. I want them to have the rewards

---

[62] Richardson 9756; Drawn from Coolidge's Address to the Pan-American Conference in Havana, Cuba, January 16, 1928.

of their own industry. This is the chief meaning of freedom."[63]

32. Govern as Campaigned

As Mayor of Northampton and throughout service in local government, Coolidge was an attentive public servant and his attention to detail made him one of the most successful vote-getters of his era. He never took anyone for granted, as Robert Woods summarizes, "He made a special point of going about freely among the citizens in order to learn their needs and hopes, and thus from day to day serve them more effectually...He followed out the method, originally practiced in Northampton, of making personal calls on many persons of influence locally...There had always been a Coolidge Democratic following in the Connecticut Valley...The sentiment of every section of the State seemed an open book to him, and the campaign managers were surprised after election by the accuracy of his predictions as

---

[63] Ibid 9439; From Coolidge's Acceptance Address of the Republican Nomination for President, August 14, 1924.

to the detailed vote...He said that public administration must be a matter of the heart as well as the head. He had echoed this conviction during the campaign. In his administration of the office of governor he proceeded in remarkable degree to put it into effect."[64]

33. Government Intervention

"No matter how it is disguised, the moment the Government engages in buying and selling, by that act it is fixing prices...Government control can not be divorced from political control."[65]

"The government has never shown much aptitude for real business. The Congress will not permit it to be conducted by a competent executive, but constantly intervenes. The most free, progressive and satisfactory method ever devised for the equitable distribution of property is to permit the people to care for themselves by

---

[64] Woods 55, 137.

[65] Coolidge, Foundations of the Republic 343; Address to American Farm Bureau Federation, Chicago, December 7, 1925.

conducting their own business. They have more wisdom than any government."[66]

"It is necessary always to give a great deal of thought to liberty. There is no substitute for it. Nothing else is quite so effective. Unless it be preserved, there is little else that is worth while. In complete freedom of action the people oftentimes have a more effective remedy than can be supplied by government interference. Individual initiative, in the long run, is a firmer reliance than bureaucratic supervision. When the people work out their own economic and social destiny, they generally reach sound conclusions."[67]

"This general principle of passing one piece of legislation at a time is most salutary. It prevents crowding through measures that the majority does not favor and forces all bills to stand on their merits."[68]

---

[66] Lathem, Calvin Coolidge Says 231; Column from January 5, 1931.

[67] Coolidge, Price of Freedom 390; From speech given by Coolidge at Wheaton College, Norton, Massachusetts, June 19, 1923.

[68] Lathem, Calvin Coolidge Says 241; Column from January 16, 1931.

34. Government Spending

"When the country needs the courage and confidence that relief from high taxes would give, increasing appropriations only add to the discouragement. What a refreshing spectacle it would be if a little band of officeholders would announce they were ready to risk defeat by resisting unsound proposals! The whole country would rally to their support."[69]

"One of the most astounding spectacles is the complacency with which people permit themselves to be plundered by extravagant governmental expenditure under the pretense of taxing the rich to help the poor. The poor are not helped but hurt...They are collected from all people...Unless the people resist vigorously and immediately they will be overwhelmed."[70]

35. Grassroots Support

While Coolidge came to national renown as a result of his decisive leadership through

---

[69] Ibid 223; Column from December 26, 1930.
[70] Ibid 273; Column from February 23, 1931.

the Boston Police Strike in 1919, he was little regarded by the Party establishment of his day, led essentially by Senator Henry Cabot Lodge. Coolidge was, however, the grassroots choice, as the election of 1920 reveals. He was not only supported by a devoted corps of delegates but Mrs. Alexandra Carlisle Pfeiffer, the only woman in the Massachusetts delegation, delivered the speech seconding Cal's nomination for President. It was when the selection of a Vice Presidential nominee came that the GOP leadership lost control of convention proceedings and a spontaneous and genuine stampede to nominate Coolidge took place from the floor.[71]

The election of 1924 mobilized that grassroots army to stellar results. While Coolidge did not participate in either of the Republican conventions, and campaigned even less in 1924, his neighbors from old Plymouth Notch took it upon themselves to bring Cal to the country. They did so through a 56-day, 6500-mile, 300-city, 17-

[71] Pietrusza, 1920: The Year of the Six Presidents (New York: Carroll & Graf Publishers, 2007) 215-216, 238-241; Coolidge, Autobiography 146.

state speaking tour along the Lincoln Highway (U. S. 30) involving folks from all over the country starting from Plymouth, Vermont, and ending in Bellingham, Washington, including countless points in between in what was dubbed, the "Coolidge-Dawes Lincoln Tour."

It brought Coolidge to the country with what newspapers called the "largest continuous procession of any kind in all history" and helped win a landslide through the grassroots.[72]

36. Greatness: Confidence and Humility

"The great man is he who can express the unuttered opinions of his time, direct energy along profitable channels, divine the spirit of the people, and unify action under just and stable institutions of government."[73] While

---

[72] Larry L. Krug, back cover, The 1924 Coolidge-Dawes Lincoln Tour. Atlgen, PA: Schiffer, 2007.

[73] Robert J. Thompson, Adequate Brevity: A Collation and Co-ordination of the Mental Processes and Reactions of Calvin Coolidge, as Expressed in his Addresses and Messages, and Constituting a Self Delineation of his Character and Ideals (Chicago: M.

Coolidge did not regard himself as such a man, he was. Whiting elaborates one of many occasions which illustrated these qualities in Cal, "[T]he Governor of an American State had asserted...that 'the authority of the Commonwealth cannot be intimidated or coerced. It cannot be compromised.' He did not argue the case; he stated a truth. In the light of after events it may appear to have been a very simple thing to do. None other had done it. The police strike provided a theatrical situation. Governor Coolidge plucked from it and gave to the American people a vital truth, the obviousness of which had been forgotten...The people suddenly saw that the Governor of an American State could and would uphold – even at the risk of his political future – law, order, and government. It was precisely this reassurance for which they had been waiting...This was a permanent impression on the public mind...That is why the national belief in him did not flag after the close of the incident of the police strike itself. Other men, governors, and statesmen, have met acute

A. Donohue & Company, 1924) 44.

crises with courage. What Coolidge did was much more. He restored national confidence in the authority of government. It was inevitable that he should become a national figure, and it was not surprising that he remained one."[74]

"It is a great advantage to a President, and a major source of safety to the country, for him to know that he is not a great man. When a man begins to feel that he is the only one who can lead in this republic, he is guilty of treason to the spirit of our institutions."[75]

" 'Mr. Coolidge, what was the first thought that came into your mind when you were told that Mr. Harding was dead and that the Presidency was yours?' Thinking a moment, Mr. Coolidge, without changing his expression in the slightest, said, 'I thought I could swing it.' "[76] Yet this was no arrogant boast, as biographer Claude Fuess points out,

---

[74] Edward Elwell Whiting, Calvin Coolidge: A Contemporary Estimate (Boston: The Atlantic Monthly, 1923) 150-151.

[75] Coolidge, Autobiography 173.
[76] Fuess 311.

Coolidge had served a "long apprenticeship in subordinate offices, had learned the science of government, both theoretical and practical, and had mastered the technique of effective administration. As he repeatedly said later, 'I was ready.' " Yet, Cal abhorred condescension and "putting on airs," being ever ready to deflate this kind of false importance both toward himself and when manifested by others.[77]

37. Honesty

"No system of government can stand that lacks public confidence and no progress can be made on the assumption of a false premise."[78]

"I am not one of those who believe votes are to be won by misrepresentations, skillful presentations of half-truths, and plausible

---

[77] Ibid 485-486; Charles Willis Thompson, <u>Presidents I've Known and Two Near Presidents</u> (Indianapolis: Bobbs-Merrill Company, 1929) 347-348.

[78] Coolidge, <u>Have Faith in Massachusetts</u> 75; Taken from an undated essay entitled, "On the Nature of Politics."

deductions from false premises. Good government cannot be found on the bargain-counter."[79]

38. Ideals

"The Government itself, in order to be successful, and all of those connected with it, must put all of their energy upon what they can do for the people, not upon what they can get out of them...Fundamentally, America is sound. It has both the power and disposition to maintain itself in a healthy economic and moral condition. But it can not do this by turning all its thoughts in on itself, or by making its material prosperity its supreme choice. Selfishness is only another name for suicide. A nation that is morally dead will soon be financially dead. The progress of the world rests on courage, honor and faith. If America wishes to maintain its prosperity, it must maintain its ideals."[80]

---

[79] Ibid 38; Address at Riverside, Massachusetts, August 28, 1916.

[80] Richardson 9396-9397; Annual Luncheon of the Associated Press, New York City, April 22, 1924.

39. Immigration

"New arrivals should be limited to our capacity to absorb them into the ranks of good citizenship...We should find additional safety in a law requiring the immediate registration of all aliens. Those who do not want to be partakers of the American spirit ought not to settle in America."[81]

40. International Conflict

"While we wish for peace everywhere, it is our desire that it should be not a peace imposed by America, but a peace established by each nation for itself...We have sufficient reserve resources so that we need not be hasty in asserting our rights. We can afford to let our patience be commensurate with our power."[82]

---

[81] Ibid 9351; Coolidge's First Annual Message, delivered before Joint Session of Congress, December 6, 1923.
[82] Ibid 9701; Speech delivered at Arlington National Cemetery, May 30, 1927.

41. Interests

"The people who start to elect a man to get what he can for his district will probably find they have elected a man who will get what he can for himself."[83]

42. Justice

"Let justice and the economic laws be applied to the strong; but for the weak there must be mercy and charity; not the gratuity which pauperizes, but the assistance which restores. That, too, is justice."[84]

"Courts are established, not to determine the popularity of a cause, but to adjudicate and enforce rights. No litigant should be required to submit his case to the hazard and expense of a political campaign. No judge should be required to seek or receive political rewards."[85]

---

[83] Coolidge, Have Faith in Massachusetts 79.

[84] Coolidge, Price of Freedom 80; Address at the Community-Chest Dinner, Springfield, Massachusetts, October 11, 1921.

[85] Coolidge, Have Faith in Massachusetts 4-5; Coolidge delivered this speech upon being elected President of the Massachusetts Senate, January 7, 1914.

43. Kindness

Confusing reticence with insensitivity, some have accused Cal of being cold and mean-spirited, yet Coolidge's kindness of heart and generosity of spirit would come in ample measure to many, including unsuspecting strangers, without ever flaunting it. When a young man crept into their room at the New Willard Hotel in the middle of the night, Cal not only talked him out of his theft, he loaned him the $32 train fare to get back to school. Cal called it a "loan" so that obligation would remain. The youngster later repaid the loan in full. This was no random kindness, Coolidge was known for writing checks to those he knew were in need from time to time, especially as the Depression took hold.

He loved children and while he never witnessed the arrival of his granddaughters, he made a point of welcoming young people to the White House, even to a visit with the President. He invited a local child to the summer White House in the Adirondacks when the young man's birthday coincided with his own. Suzanne Boone, the three-year-old daughter of his physician, was a frequent guest of the President and First Lady. His Secret Service agent, Colonel Starling, recounts the time he noticed a boy peering onto the grounds from outside the fence, seeking to comfort the President after the loss of his youngest boy. Coolidge, deeply moved by the sentiment, received the lad and instructed Starling to never turn away another child who had come to see the President.[86]

The President never "joined" organizations to simply win support. His steadfast rule never to subscribe his name and influence to organizations of any kind found one exception: when the entity was actually performing real good to the people it was created to help. This was the case with the American Federation for the Blind led by Helen Keller. There is a wonderful exchange

[86] "Coolidge Loaned Money to His Hotel-Room Thief," The Dispatch 6 August 1983 <https://news.google.com/newspapers?nid=1734&dat=19830806&id=64EcAAAAIBAJ&sjid=f1IEAAAAIBAJ&pg=5743,3927086&hl=en>; Grace Coolidge, "The Real Calvin Coolidge," Good Housekeeping June 1935: 204; Starling 224.

between Mrs. Coolidge and Helen Keller after visiting the President, during which she read his lips with her fingers.

GC to HK: "The President thought I was the only woman in the world who knew he had a warm heart and you seemed to sense it the moment you touched his hand."

HK to GC: "I feel in the hand what the eye cannot see...I knew the President was really glad to see me. Your dear husband thinks many things he doesn't tell to everyone and there are wonderful things in his heart."[87]

Coolidge's favorite portrait painter was Ercole Cartotto, who completed three official oil portraits and numerous sketches over the course of three years. Among artists, few came to consider the President as real a friend as Mr. Cartotto did. He said of Coolidge, "I was privileged to know him gradually as the humane, friendly, deliberate, and balanced person that he was—solid as the granite of his state, and yet as gentle a

[87] "Mrs. Coolidge Happy Miss Keller, Too, Found the President's Heart," Boston Herald 12 January 1926.

human being, free from all frills and veneer, as one could meet."[88]

44. Law

"Men do not make laws. They do but discover them. Laws must be justified by something more than the will of the majority. They must rest on the eternal foundation of righteousness"...

"The people cannot look to legislation generally for success. Industry, thrift, character, are not conferred by act or resolve. Government cannot relieve from toil"...

"The normal must care for themselves. Self-government means self-support"...

"Do the day's work. If it be to protect the rights of the weak, whoever objects, do it. If it be to help a powerful corporation better to serve the people, whatever the opposition, do that. Expect to be called a standpatter, but don't be a standpatter. Expect to be

[88] Ercole Cartotto, "In Defense of a 'Foreign' Painter," Good Housekeeping March 1935: 223.

called a demagogue, but don't be a demagogue. Don't hesitate to be a revolutionary as science. Don't hesitate to be as reactionary as the multiplication table. Don't expect to build up the weak by pulling down the strong. Don't hurry to legislate. Give administration a chance to catch up with legislation"...

"Statutes must appeal to more than material welfare. Wages won't satisfy, be they never so large. Nor houses; nor lands; no coupons, though they fall thick as the leaves of autumn. Man has a spiritual nature. Touch it, and it must respond as the magnet responds to the pole. To that, not to selfishness, let the laws of the Commonwealth appeal. Recognize the immortal worth and dignity of man."[89]

45. Legislation

"You need not hesitate to give the other members your views on any subject that arises. It is much more important to kill bad

---

[89] Coolidge, Have Faith in Massachusetts 4, 5, 7-9; Inaugural Address as Senate President, January 7, 1914.

bills than to pass good ones, and better to spend your time on your own committee work than by bothering with any bills of your own except in some measure that your own County or some other persons may want you to introduce for them...See that bills you recommend from your committee are so worded that they will do just what they intend and not a great deal more that is undesirable. Most bills can't stand that test."[90]

46. Local Government

"What we need is not more Federal government, but better local government...When the local government unit evades its responsibility in one direction, it is started in the vicious way of disregard of law and laxity of living...If we are too weak to take charge of our own morality, we shall not be strong enough to take charge of our own liberty. If we can not govern ourselves, if we can not observe the law,

[90] Lathem, ed., Your Son, Calvin Coolidge: A Selection of Letters from Calvin Coolidge to his Father (Montpelier: Vermont Historical Society, 1968) 117; Letter to his father, September 6, 1910, upon Colonel Coolidge's election to the Vermont Senate.

nothing remains but to have some one else govern us, to have the law enforced against us, and to step down from the honorable abiding place of freedom to the ignominious abode of servitude."[91]

"It seemed to me that the towns in this commonwealth correspond in part to what we might call the water-tight compartments of the ship of state, and while sometimes our state government has wavered...whenever that has arisen, the towns of the commonwealth have come to the rescue."[92]

"State legislatures are fresh from the people. They know the conditions of their own neighborhoods much better than Congressmen know them."[93]

---

[91] Coolidge, Foundations of the Republic 228, 229, 231; Address given at Arlington National Cemetery, May 30, 1925.

[92] Coolidge, Have Faith in Massachusetts 91; At the Dedication of Town-House, Weston, Massachusetts, November 27, 1917.

[93] Lathem, Calvin Coolidge Says 235; Column from January 9, 1931.

47. Love for People

Thomas A. Buckner, with whom former President Coolidge collaborated in service to the New York Life Insurance Company, saw Cal's heart to pitch in and help when someone had a need. Being a former President of the United States, surely he could have made use of any number of excuses not to lend a hand, roll up sleeves and run an errand, however menial.

Yet, Coolidge retained a lasting sense of humility, even after years in high political office. Mr. Buckner says, "Those of us who came near to Mr. Coolidge knew that his reserve and taciturnity covered a generous nature which might otherwise have been imposed upon by self-seekers. He was always willing to lend a helping hand to others, no matter how humble. For example, one day Mr. Coolidge entered our home office carrying an enormous bundle. He explained that a young man from Newark would call for it and that it would be returned a month hence, at which time Mr. Coolidge would pick it up. The size of the bundle aroused the curiosity of Miss Morris, secretary to Mr.

Kingsley, and she asked Mr. Coolidge what it contained. He explained that an ambitious young man had entered a contest for window displays, and that he had asked for something from the old Vermont farm. Although the young man did not know Mr. Coolidge personally, his enterprise evidently carried a strong appeal. Mr. Coolidge had therefore carried to New York and generously loaned a bed quilt made by his grandmother many years ago. Calvin Coolidge had a deep love for humanity. He is greatly missed, but his spirit remains with us."[94]

"On one occasion I shook hands with nineteen hundred in thirty-four minutes, which is probably my record. Instead of a burden, it was a pleasure and a relief to meet people in that way and listen to their greeting, which was often a benediction."[95]

---

[94] Thomas A. Buckner, "Why Director Coolidge Carried A Quilt," Good Housekeeping April 1935: 200.
[95] Coolidge, Autobiography 203.

48. Loyalty

Too often politics descends into a quest to advance, stepping on whomever one has to, in the name of expedience, to reach the next goal. Coolidge opposed this debasing of public service. He cherished the friendship of faithful men and women with whom he collaborated over the course of thirty years in elective office. He never forgot the good folks who helped him in various ways, campaigned for him, and served well in his administrations. Perhaps most importantly, they never forgot him and retained loyalty to Cal the rest of his life. C. Bascom Slemp was such a friend. Coolidge writes him after the outcome of the 1932 elections, which went badly for their party and would bode ill for the country in the coming years. The former President writes his former Secretary, "I am glad that you and I are not in politics during these terrible times. I retired at the right time and am more and more thankful every day, but because I do not want to be in politics is no reason why I do not want to see my old friends. If I could have them about me as they were in Washington, my satisfaction in life would be complete."⁹⁶

49. Majority vs. Minority

"We have never seen, and it is unlikely that we ever shall see, the time when we can safely relax our vigilance and risk our institutions to run themselves under the hand of an active, even though well-intentioned, minority...No minority is good enough to be trusted with the government of a majority...We shall be wise if we maintain also that no majority can be trusted to be wise enough and good enough, at all times, to exercise unlimited control over a minority. We need the restraints of a written constitution."[97]

50. Making Speeches

"I don't recall any candidate for President that ever injured himself very much by not

---

[96] Calvin Coolidge, letter to C. Bascom Slemp, 29 December 1932, C. Bascom Slemp Papers, 1866-1944, Accession #9507, Special Collections Department, University of Virginia Library, Charlottesville, Virginia.
[97] Excerpt from Coolidge's Address to the Thirty-Third Continental Congress of the Daughters of the American Revolution, April 14, 1924.

talking."[98] Yet, Coolidge also made plain the intense effort that he poured into crafting his own speeches, when he says, "This kind of work is very exacting...It is not difficult for me to deliver an address. The difficulty lies in its preparation. This is an important part of the work of a President which he can not escape. It is inherent in the office."[99] This, at least partly, is why he resisted efforts to "draft" him back into office in 1932, telling painter Ercole Cartotto as he pointed to the collection of his speeches, "Those are my works of art...Every word in them had to be considered for fear of misuse. The drudgery, the attention they required, is too much of a strain to do over again."[100]

---

[98] Quint, Howard, and Robert Ferrell, eds. The Talkative President: The Off-the Record Press Conferences of Calvin Coolidge (Amherst: University of Massachusetts, 1964) 10; Referencing a press conference from September 16, 1924.

[99] Coolidge, Autobiography 221.
[100] Cartotto 223.

51. Materialism

"We live in an age of science and of abounding accumulation of material things. These did not create our Declaration. Our Declaration created them. The things of the spirit come first. Unless we cling to that, all our material prosperity, overwhelming though it may appear, will turn to a barren scepter in our grasp. If we are to maintain the great heritage which has been bequeathed to us, we must be like-minded as the fathers who created it. We must not sink into a pagan materialism...We must follow the spiritual and moral leadership which they showed."[101]

52. Military Preparedness

"I am not unfamiliar with the claim that if only we had a sufficient military establishment no one would ever molest us. I know of no nation in history that has ever been able to attain that position. I see no

---

[101] Coolidge, <u>Foundations of the Republic</u> 454; From his speech at the Sesquicentennial celebrations in Philadelphia for the Declaration of Independence, July 5, 1926.

reason to expect that we could be the exception. Although I believe thoroughly in adequate military preparations, what I am trying to argue is that they are not sufficient unto themselves. I do not believe the American Navy can succeed if it represents mere naked force. I want to see it represent much more than that. We must place it on a much higher plane. We must make it an instrument of righteousness. If we are to promote peace on earth, we must have a great deal more than the power of the sword. We must call into action the spiritual and moral forces of mankind."[102]

"We have all nourished a commendable sentiment of moderate preparation for national defense, believing that for a nation to be unreasonably neglectful of the military art, even if it did not invite and cause such aggression as to result either in war or in abject humiliation, it must finally lead to a disastrous disintegration of the very moral fiber of the nation."[103]

---

[102] Ibid 243-244; From Coolidge's Address to the graduating class of the U. S. Naval Academy, Annapolis, June 3, 1925.
[103] Richardson 9756; Address before the Pan-

53. Negative Campaigning

It is little known that Mr. Coolidge once served as Chairman for his local Party's Committee in Northampton. While he secured success for candidates statewide in 1904, he was unsuccessful in helping the candidate for Mayor win his election. Coolidge, writing years later, explained what he learned from that pivotal experience, "We made the mistake of talking too much about the deficiencies of our opponents and not enough about the merits of our own candidates. I have never again fallen into that error."[104] It is not enough to give voters something against which to vote, they must be given something for which to vote and someone for whom to vote.

"He hurled no epithets at his opponents, when they made false statements about him and his administration, but simply declared: 'They are in error,' and pointed out how they had been misinformed."[105]

American Conference, Havana, Cuba, January 16, 1928.

[104] Coolidge, Autobiography 91.

54. Partisanship

"While an independent attitude on the part of the citizen is not without a certain public advantage, yet it is necessary under our form of government to have political parties. Unless some one is a partisan, no one can be an independent."[106]

55. Party Principles

"Common honesty and good faith with the people who support a party at the polls require that party, when it enters office, to assume the control of that portion of the Government to which it has been elected. Any other course is bad faith and a violation of the party pledges. When the country has bestowed its confidence upon a party by making it a majority in the Congress, it has a right to expect such unity of action as will make the party majority an effective instrument of government."[107]

---

[105] Hennessy 60.

[106] Coolidge, Autobiography 230-231.

[107] Coolidge, Foundations of the Republic 200;

56. Patriotism

"There is no substitute for a militant freedom. The only alternative is submission and slavery."[108]

57. Pay Increase

"To the Honorable Senate and House of Representatives...Service in the General Court is not obligatory but optional. It is not to be undertaken as a profession or a means of livelihood. It is a voluntary public service...Membership in the General Court is not a job...For the searching out of great principles on which legislation is based there is no adequate compensation...Men do not serve here for pay. They seek work and places of responsibility and find in that seeking, not in their pay, their honor...No

---

Excerpt of his Inaugural Address, March 4, 1925.

[108] Coolidge, Price of Freedom 159; From his Address at the Dedication of the Monument in honor of General Ulysses Grant, Washington, D.C., April 27, 1922.

person was ever honored for what he received. Honor has been the reward for what he gave...Not by indulging himself, but by denying himself, will he reach success."[109]

58. Peace

"In spite of all the treaties we may make and all the tribunals we may establish, unless we maintain a public opinion devoted to peace we can not escape the ravages of war. A determination to do right will be more effective than all our treaties and courts, all our armies and fleets. A peaceful people will have peace, but a warlike people can not escape war."[110]

59. Perspective

"It is characteristic of the unlearned that they are forever proposing something which

---

[109] Coolidge, Have Faith in Massachusetts 171-174; From Governor Coolidge's veto of a salary increase by the General Court.

[110] Coolidge, Foundations of the Republic 432; From his Address at Arlington National Cemetery, May 31, 1926.

is old, and because it has recently come to their own attention, supposing it to be new."[111]

" 'Mr. President,' I asked, 'what do you think of ministers trying to influence legislation?' 'I don't know,' Mr. Coolidge...responded. 'I used to have close contact with that sort of thing when I was in the Massachusetts legislature, but I didn't know so much about it when I was down at Washington...I recall, Mr. Sneed, a sentence by an old writer to the effect that "Jesus Christ never spent any time in the lobby of the Caesars.' In other words, Jesus did not depend for the advancement of His kingdom and His principles upon such means...'How long have you preached, Mr. Sneed?' asked my shrewd host. 'Only four years,' I replied...'My contribution is limited.' He looked at me understandingly, and then he made his remark which, I thought, summarized his philosophy of life: 'Yes, but multiply that two a year by twenty-five or forty years of activity, and think what you have poured into the standard of human living. It is only as we take up the burdens

[111] Coolidge, Have Faith in Massachusetts 231; From his Address at Holy Cross College, Worcester, Massachusetts, June 25, 1919.

which present themselves day by day that life holds meaning. It is by assuming these burdens regularly that one forms habits which make decisions become almost second nature and judgments easier.' "[112]

60. Political Mentors

Blessed throughout his career with good men and women with whom he came in contact, Coolidge has this to say about one he wished had still been alive when he became President, "the Honorable W. Murray Crane," United States Senator from Massachusetts. He says of Crane, "He confirmed my opinion as to the value of silence which avoids creating a situation where one would otherwise not exist, and the bad taste and the danger of advertising an opponent by making any attack on him. In all political affairs he had a wonderful wisdom, and in everything he was preeminently a man of judgment, who was the most disinterested public servant I ever saw and the greatest influence for good

---

[112] J. Richard Sneed, "Christ and the Caesars," Good Housekeeping June 1935: 198.

government with which I ever came in contact."[113]

61. Political Mind

"The political mind is the product of men in public life who have been twice spoiled. They have been spoiled with praise and they have been spoiled with abuse. With them nothing is natural, everything is artificial. A few rare souls escape these influences and maintain a vision and a judgment that are unimpaired. They are a great comfort to every President and a great service to their country."[114]

"A President should not only not be selfish, but he ought to avoid the appearance of selfishness. The people would not have confidence in a man that appeared to be grasping for office. It is difficult for men in high office to avoid the malady of self-delusion. They are always surrounded by worshippers. They are constantly, and for the most part sincerely, assured of their greatness. They live in an artificial

---

[113] Coolidge, Autobiography 113-114.
[114] Ibid 229.

atmosphere of adulation and exaltation which sooner or later impairs their judgment. They are in grave danger of becoming careless and arrogant."[115]

62. Political Parties

"The parties appeal to the voters in behalf of their platforms. The people make their choice on those issues. Unless those who are elected on the same party platform associate themselves together to carry out its provisions, the election becomes a mockery. The independent voter who has joined with others in placing a party nominee in office finds his efforts were all in vain, if the person he helps elect refuses or neglects to keep the platform pledges of his party."[116]

63. Presiding

"As a presiding officer it has constantly been my policy to dispatch business...I was able to keep the daily sessions of the Senate short. I

---

[115] Ibid 241.
[116] Ibid 230-231.

also wanted to cut down the volume of legislation. In this some progress was made. The Blue Book of Acts and Resolves for 1913 had 1,763 pages, for 1914 it has 1,423, and for 1915 only 1,230, which was a very wholesome reduction of more than thirty per cent. People were coming to see that they must depend on themselves rather than on legislation for success."[117]

"As a presiding officer he was calm and fair-minded. He had a thorough acquaintance with parliamentary procedure and was sound in his rulings. When Senator Walter E. McLane, told by an indignant colleague to go to hell, protested, Coolidge replied, 'Senator, I've examined the Constitution and the Senate rules, and there's nothing in them that compels you to go."[118]

"As President of the Senate, he had a fuller opportunity than ever before to express his capacity as a leader. Well-informed observers have stated that no man in his position in the past generation had managed

[117] Ibid 110.

[118] Fuess 122; Whiting, President Coolidge: A Contemporary Estimate 100-101.

the affairs of the Senate with more tact and with less friction. He knew how to hold a properly judicial attitude toward all proposals. He was always fair to members of the opposite party, and won their support in an unusual degree. He guided deliberations rather than shaped conclusions. Yet when the time came to expedite business, he could do it marvellously. When tactics of delay were attempted, he knew how to use the steam-roller. He kept a continuously firm grip on the whole situation, and could dispose of a clearly ill-judged measure with a word, or be just as ready to allow the fullest discussion of a measure that required to be ventilated...His way was always to lead, never to drive. He is hardly remembered to have given an order; a suggestion or intimation or some turn of Yankee wit from him accomplished more."[119]

"The ideal way for it [the Presidency] to function is to assign to the various positions men of sufficient ability so that they can solve all the problems that arise under their jurisdiction...While it is wise for the

---

[119] Woods 31-32.

President to get all the competent advice possible, final judgments are necessarily his own. No one can share with him the responsibility for them. No one can make his decisions for him. He stands at the center of things where no one else can stand...His decisions are final and usually irreparable. This constitutes the appalling burden of his office."[120]

64. Press Image

Few men have as masterfully handled press relations as Calvin Coolidge did. His 521 bi-weekly press conferences not only established the custom started under Harding, it opened a channel between the President and the Press that would exceed over a mere sixty-seven months the record of successors, including the 145-month average of FDR.[121] Coolidge understood that the press business was changing from its almost salacious exposes of earlier years to a respected participant in the business of

---

[120] Coolidge, <u>Autobiography</u> 199.
[121] Elmer E. Cornwell, Jr., <u>Presidential Leadership of Public Opinion</u> (Westport, CT: Greenwood, 1965) 74-75.

earning a profit and providing customers with the service in news coverage they sought. Journalists were beholden to the same marketplace on which the rest of the country worked rather than in defiance of it. His compassion for the working press, including the photographers, and their daily need for copy, compelled the President to go out of his way to furnish a White House at their disposal, a modern apex of news and events, a level of transparency and publicity never before known. Coolidge took press relations to an art form. Responding to the claim that he enjoyed an unfairly favorable coverage, the President said, "I suppose that I am not very good copy...But the boys have been very kind and considerate to me...They have undertaken to endow me with some characteristics and traits that I didn't altogether know I had. But I have done the best I could to be perfectly fair with them, and in public, to live up to those traits."[122]

Consequently, Coolidge could look back on his six years and say, "You have been, I think, quite successful in interpreting the

---

[122] Ibid 89.

administration to the country. I have known that I wasn't much of a success in undertaking newspaper work, so I have left the work of reporting the affairs of my administration to the experts of the Press. Perhaps that is the reason that the reports have been more successful than they would have been if I had undertaken myself to direct them. It has been a pleasure to have you come in twice a week and give me an opportunity to answer such queries as you wished to propound. I want to thank you again for your constant kindness and consideration."[123]

65. Priorities

"Financial stability is the first requisite of sound government."[124]

---

[123] Quint and Ferrell 34.
[124] Richardson 9343; From Coolidge's First Annual Message delivered before Congress, December 6, 1923.

66. Promises

"It is always very easy to promise everything. It is sometimes difficult to deliver anything. In our political and economic life there will always be those who are lavish with unwanted criticism and well supplied with false hopes. It is always well to remember that American institutions have stood the test of experience. They do not profess to promise everything, but to communities and to individuals who have been content to live by them they have never failed in their satisfactions and rewards. Here industry can find employment, thrift can amass a competency, and square dealing is assured of justice."[125]

67. Propaganda

"The public press under an autocracy is necessarily a true agency of propaganda. Under a free government it must be the very

---

[125] Everett Sanders Papers, Manuscript Division, Library of Congress, Washington, D. C.; Excerpt from Coolidge's Address at the Dedication of Wicker Memorial Park to the veterans of World War I, Hammond, Indiana, June 14, 1927.

reverse. Propaganda seeks to present a part of the facts, to distort their relations, and to force conclusions which could not be drawn from a complete and candid survey of all the facts. It has been observed that propaganda seeks to close the mind, while education seeks to open it. This has become of the dangers of the present day...Unfortunately, not all experts are completely disinterested. Not all specialists are completely without guile. In our increasing dependence on specialized authority, we tend to become easier victims for the propagandists, and need to cultivate sedulously the habit of the open mind...We need to keep our minds free of prejudice and bias. Of education and real information we cannot get too much. But of propaganda, which is tainted or perverted information, we cannot have too little."[126]

---

[126] Coolidge, Foundations of the Republic 184-185; Portion of an Address before the American Society of Newspaper Editors, Washington, D. C., January 17, 1925. This is the speech often misquoted to prove Coolidge's "worship" of Big Business (i.e., "the *chief* business of America is business"; see #5 of our collection and read this entire speech in order to better appreciate why this address is especially targeted by some to mischaracterize Cal).

68. Public Debate

"A good measure can stand discussion. A bad bill ought to be delayed...Open debate is the only shield against the irretrievable action of a rash majority."[127]

69. Public Trust

"We must have no carelessness in our dealings with public property or the expenditure of public money. Such a condition is characteristic either of an undeveloped people, or of a decadent civilization. America is neither...We must have an administration which is marked, not by the inexperience of youth, or the futility of age, but by the character and ability of maturity."[128]

"Money will not purchase character or good government."[129]

---

[127] Lathem, Calvin Coolidge Says 286; Column from March 10, 1931.

[128] Coolidge, Foundations of the Republic 46; From his Address at the Seventh Meeting of the Business Organization of the Government held in Memorial Continental Hall, Washington, D. C., June 30, 1924.

[129] Coolidge, Have Faith in Massachusetts 18; Taken

70. Reform

"Laws do not make reforms; reforms make laws. We cannot look to government. We must look to ourselves."[130]

"Error lies in supposing that great fundamental reforms can be at once accomplished by the mere passage of a law. By law is meant a rule of action. Action depends upon intelligence and motive. If either of these be lacking, the action fails and the law fails."[131]

"Real reform does not begin with a law; it ends with a law. The attempt to dragoon the body when the need is to convince the soul will end only in revolt...The law, changed and changeable on slight provocation, loses its sanctity and authority."[132]

---

from his Message to the Brockton Chamber of Commerce, April 11, 1916.

[130] Ibid 83; From Coolidge's essay, "On the Nature of Politics."

[131] Coolidge, Price of Freedom 293; From his Address before the New York State Convention of the Y.M.C.A., Albany, April 13, 1923.

[132] Ibid 206-207; Address before the American Bar Association, San Francisco, August 10, 1922.

71. Regulation

"We have had many attempts at regulation of industrial activity by law. Some of it has proceeded on the theory that if those who enjoyed material prosperity used it for wrong purposes, such prosperity should be limited or abolished. That is as sound as it would be to abolish writing to prevent forgery. We need to keep forever in mind that guilt is personal; if there is to be punishment let it fall on the evil-doer, let us not condemn the instrument."[133]

72. Religion

"The government of a country never gets ahead of the religion of a country. There is no way by which we can substitute the authority of law for the virtue of man. Of course we can help to restrain the vicious and furnish a fair degree of security and protection by legislation and police control, but the real reforms which society in these

---

[133] Coolidge, Have Faith in Massachusetts 64-65; Address at Associated Industries Dinner, Boston, December 15, 1916.

days is seeking will come as a result of our religious convictions, or they will not come at all."[134]

73. Residency

"We liked the house where our children came to us and the neighbors who were so kind. When we could have had a more pretentious home we still clung to it. So long as I lived there, I could be independent and serve the public without ever thinking that I could not maintain my position if I lost my office. I always made my living practicing law up to the time I became Governor, without being dependent on any official salary. This left me free to make my own decisions in accordance with what I thought was the public good. We lived where we did that I might better serve the people."[135]

---

[134] Coolidge, Foundations of the Republic 153; Address at the unveiling of the Equestrian Statute of Bishop Francis Asbury, Washington, D. C., October 15, 1924.
[135] Coolidge, Autobiography 96.

74. Results

Frank W. Stearns would first meet the future President in 1914 and correspondent Morton Berg recounts his initial reaction to then-Senator Coolidge, "You can imagine then when I felt when that man (Coolidge) sat through our plea without saying a word, without moving a facial muscle. When we were through he not only failed to endorse our little bill, he failed to say that he was sorry that he could not explain why. Do you wonder, then, that I spent nearly a year being angry at Coolidge? It turned out later that the...bill had been presented too late in the year to be considered at that session. But no matter. I could never forgive him, I felt. The surprise of my life came the next session. Coolidge, who had become president of the Massachusetts Senate, made it his business at the earliest possible moment to put through our bill. He did it unsolicited. Moreover, he incorporated valuable amendments which had not occurred to us the year before. Of course this changed my attitude toward Calvin Coolidge. It interested me in the man. First, I sought his acquaintance, then his friendship."[136]

Stearns was amazed and for the next decade touted Coolidge's qualifications for higher office, all the way to the White House. Roland Sawyer, in his biography of Coolidge, echoes that observation about the man, saying, "It was his habit to make the next visitor wait while his secretary was called and the wheels were set in motion on the thing wanted. Such treatment was so unusual in an office-holder that Mr. Coolidge soon had a lot of smaller 'Frank Stearnses' rooting for him."[137] As biographer Horace Green notes, "The story is, in the main, interesting because typical of the Coolidge method of action, a method originally natural and developed because of its success...The method is to to put the worst foot forward, discourage hope, promise nothing. The resultant action, if it does come, and especially if it is reported to the beneficiary through a roundabout source, is an unforgettable surprise."[138]

---

[136] Horace Green, The Life of Calvin Coolidge (New York: Duffield & Company, 1924) 94-95.

[137] Sawyer 63.

[138] Green 95.

75. Retirement

"I do not choose to run for President in nineteen twenty-eight."[139]

It is indeed a rare thing when leaders, having held power, put it down voluntarily and walk away. Returning to private life is all the more extraordinary because Coolidge would certainly have won reelection unchallenged and remained eligible for another four years. He considered ten years far too long for any one man to stay in office. The country needed someone new, a candidate they, not he, should choose. With that characteristic dry humor and shrewd political sense, he once told a member of his Cabinet, shortly before leaving the Presidency, "It is a pretty good idea to get out when they still want

---

[139] Everett Sanders Papers, Manuscript Division, Library of Congress, Washington, D. C.; Included among the Sanders' Papers is the original handwritten slip of paper of which copies were presented at a special press conference on the fourth anniversary of his renowned Homestead Inauguration (August 2, 1927) to the correspondents awaiting what was assumed to be some routine statement by President Coolidge. The actual news shocked the country.

you."[140] Urged later by friends to run again in order to end the Depression, Cal retorted, "It would be the beginning of mine."[141]

76. Rightness

"The right thing to do never requires subterfuge, it is always simple and direct."[142]

77. Running for Office

"Naturally the question arises, what shall we do to defend our birthright? In the first place everybody must take a more active part in public affairs. It will not do for men to send, they must go. It is not enough to draw a check. Good government cannot be bought, it has to be given...Unless good citizens hold office bad citizens will."[143]

---

[140] Grace Coolidge, "The Real Calvin Coolidge," Good Housekeeping May 1935: 255.

[141] Otis Skinner, "A Depression Even More Depressing," Good Housekeeping February 1935: 189.

[142] Coolidge, Autobiography 133.

[143] Coolidge, Have Faith in Massachusetts 271; Speech given at Tremont Temple, November 1, 1919.

78. Running on Own Merits

"You know that I would not relish making any attack on the opposition candidate. My entire training has been in speaking when I had some authority back of my word. I was effective because I could tell what I proposed to do."[144]

79. Scapegoats

"I do not propose to sacrifice any innocent man for my own welfare, nor do I propose to retain in office any unfit man for my own welfare. I shall try to maintain the functions of the government unimpaired, to act upon the evidence and the law as I find it, and to deal thoroughly and summarily with every kind of wrongdoing."[145]

---

[144] Calvin Coolidge, letter to Edward T. Clark 26 September 1932, Edward T. Clark Papers, Manuscript Division, Library of Congress, Washington, D. C.

[145] Richardson 9366-9367; Part of a statement by President Coolidge upon passage of a Senate Resolution for the Resignation of Navy Secretary Edwin Denby, February 11, 1924.

80. Self-Government

"There are always those who are willing to surrender local self-government and turn over their affairs to some national authority in exchange for a payment of money out of the Federal Treasury. Whenever they find that some abuse needs correction in their neighborhood, instead of applying a remedy themselves they seek to have a tribunal sent on from Washington to discharge their duties for them, regardless of the fact that in accepting such supervision they are bartering away their freedom. Such actions are always taken on the assumption that they are a public benefit. Somewhere, Lincoln said something to the effect that tyrants always bestrode the necks of the people upon the plea that it was for their good. He might have added that the people suffered the rule of tyranny in the hope that it would be easier than to rule themselves. We have built our institutions around the rights of the individual. We believe he will be better off if he looks after himself. We believe that the municipality, the State, and the National will each be better off if they look after themselves."[146]

"We demand entire freedom of action and then expect the government in some miraculous way to save us from the consequences of our own acts...If we continue the more reasonable practice of managing our own affairs we must bear the burdens of our own mistakes. A free people cannot shift their responsibility for them to the government."[147]

81. Sense of Humor

After an especially long-winded opponent concluded his arguments regarding the bill under discussion, having began each point with the phrase, "It is." Coolidge, as a young state representative, took the floor to respond, "Mr. Speaker: It isn't" -- and then sat down. The point was made and the bill went down in defeat.[148]

---

[146] Everett Sanders Papers, Manuscript Division, Library of Congress, Washington, D. C.; Address before the Society of the Daughters of the American Revolution, Washington, D. C., April 16, 1928.

[147] Lathem, Calvin Coolidge Says 163; Column from October 17, 1930.

[148] Cameron Rogers, The Legend of Calvin Coolidge (Garden City, NY: Doubleday, Doran & Company,

On one of his morning walks, Coolidge and Senator Selden Spencer of Missouri were returning to the White House, and the Senator, pointing to the historic residence, joked, "I wonder who lives there?

Coolidge: "Nobody. They just come and go."[149]

Voter in 1910: "I didn't vote for you."

Coolidge: "Well, somebody did." Coolidge had just won election as Mayor of Northampton, one of twenty-one times his name would be placed before the people for consideration.[150]

When once asked whether he had any hobbies, the President responded without breaking a smile, "Holding office."[151]

1928) 129.

[149] Fuess 479.
[150] Robert Sobel, Coolidge: An American Enigma (Washington, D. C.: Regnery, 1998) 72.
[151] John Hiram McKee, Coolidge Wit and Wisdom: 125 Short Stories About "Cal" (New York: Frederick A. Stokes, 1933) 66; Fuess 106.

Serving from Ward committeeman to Vice President, Coolidge came to the White House with more small-town, practical government experience than most of our Presidents. Yet, each promotion did not spoil him; he kept his humility and retired from public life in 1929 the same man.

When informed, after retiring from public life, that Congress had just purchased an ornate Gutenberg Bible for an exorbitant amount of public money, Coolidge wryly observed, "I should think that an ordinary copy of the King James version would have been good enough for those Congressmen."[152]

82. Service

"So much emphasis has been put upon the false that the significance of the true has been obscured and politics has come to convey the meaning of crafty and cunning selfishness, instead of candid and sincere service."[153]

---

[152] Fuess 483-484.

[153] Coolidge, Have Faith in Massachusetts 69; From "On the Nature of Politics."

"We are the possessors of tremendous power, both as individuals and as states. The great question of the preservation of our institutions is a moral question. Shall we use our power for self-aggrandizement or for service?"[154]

83. Setting the Example

Frank W. Stearns recounts this incident, reminding us that political rank does not exempt one from the rules, rather it requires living up to a higher example others can follow. Stearns notes of Coolidge, "His respect for office was tied up with a really unassuming modesty. I remember his rebuke to Horrigan, one of our state policemen who was his bodyguard while Governor. Horrigan, a fine man and proud of his assignment, had stopped traffic for him as

---

[154] Peter Hannaford, ed., <u>The Quotable Calvin Coolidge: Sensible Words for a New Century</u> (Bennington, VT: Images from the Past, 2001) 109; Part of the speech delivered by Vice President-elect Coolidge to the Vermont Historical Society and members of his native state's House of Representatives, January 18, 1921.

they left the hotel after luncheon one day. Mr. Coolidge said: 'If there should be an emergency call for me, I suppose I would have the right to stop traffic. But don't do it otherwise. I am the first person in Massachusetts to obey the law, not the last.' "[155]

84. Solvency

Bruce Barton: "Governor, how it is that you have been able to stay in public life all these years and hold office when you have no money?"

Calvin Coolidge: "I'm solvent."

Bruce Barton: "He took care to keep solvent. He never lost his head. He never let anything change him."[156]

"It is difficult to conceive a person finding himself in a situation which calls on him to maintain a position he cannot pay for. Any

---

[155] Frank W. Stearns, "Why His Poker Face," Good Housekeeping May 1935: 247.

[156] McKee x; Portion of radio address originally given by Bruce Barton, carried by stations of the National Broadcasting Company, on the night of Coolidge's death, January 5, 1933.

other course for me would have been cut short by the barnyard philosophy of my father, who would have contemptuously referred to such action as the senseless imitation of a fowl which was attempting to light higher than it could roost. There is no dignity quite so impressive as living within your means."[157]

85. States' Rights

"The States should not be induced by coercion or by favor to surrender the management of their own affairs...On the other hand...The doctrine of State rights is not a privilege to continue in wrong-doing but a privilege to be free from interference in well-doing."[158]

"Under our National Government the States are the sheet-anchors of our institutions. On them falls the task of administering local affairs and of supporting the National Government in peace and war."[159]

---

[157] Coolidge, Autobiography 158.
[158] Coolidge, Foundations of the Republic 411; From his speech at the College of William and Mary, Williamsburg, Virginia, May 15, 1926.

86. Straight Answers

"The outstanding characteristic of Calvin Coolidge as President was that no visitor to the Executive Offices who had a right to his opinion ever left his presence in doubtful mind. Coolidge never dodged. With many Presidents, as with other high officials at Washington, it is the habit to allow visitors clamoring for approval of their pet projects to wear themselves out week after week awaiting a decision already made. Coolidge in his quiet but firm way never allowed his visitors thus to deceive themselves. Moreover, there were no 'ifs' or 'buts' in his replies. He never spoke until he was sure; then he spoke definitely. On several occasions when I complimented him on an address he had made, or on one of his vetoes, he would say: 'Oh, there's nothing to that. It's just the common sense of it. There is no need of profound study to reach most of the decisions we have to make in life. Just

[159] Coolidge, <u>Have Faith in Massachusetts</u> 154; Address given at Tremont Temple, November 2, 1918.

get to the heart of it, and figure straight from there.' "[160]

87. Strategy

"I have seen a great many attempts at political strategy in my day and elaborate plans made to encompass the destruction of this or that public man. I cannot now think of any that did not react with overwhelming force upon the perpetrators, sometimes destroying them and sometimes giving their proposed victim an opportunity to demonstrate his courage, strength and soundness, which increased his standing with the people and raised him to higher office. There is only form of political strategy in which I have any confidence, and that is to try to do the right thing and sometimes to succeed."[161]

"Unless the nomination came to me in a natural way, rather than as the result of an artificial campaign, I did not feel it would be of any value."[162]

---

[160] Henry Stoddard, "Hands Off Mexico," Good Housekeeping May 1935: 250.
[161] Coolidge, Autobiography 189.

Looking back on the 1928 Presidential campaign, Coolidge had this word of caution to splitting the vote between several candidates in the hopes of defeating frontrunners. It was a lesson he had seen fail before when Theodore Roosevelt helped give the election to Democrat Woodrow Wilson by splitting the vote in the Republican Party. Cal writes,

"A strong group of the party in and outside of the Senate made the mistake of undertaking to oppose Mr. Hoover with a large number of local candidates, which finally resulted in their not developing enough strength for any particular candidate to make a showing sufficient to impress the convention."[163]

88. Substance

"When you substitute patronage for patriotism, administration breaks down. We need more of the Office Desk and less of the

---

[162] Ibid 190.
[163] Ibid 245-246.

Show Window in politics. Let men in office substitute the midnight oil for the limelight."[164]

89. Take Charge or Don't Run

When friend and former personal secretary, Ted Clark, confided that FDR was considering a coalition Cabinet in the months leading up the election of 1932, with Coolidge as a possible central figure in the new administration, Cal wrote back to Mr. Clark, "The latter part of it sounds preposterous to me, excepting for the fact that the person involved appears to be all things to all men. If he does not feel able to handle the situation with his own associates he ought to tell the country so in order that they might get a man who can."[165] As Edward Ranson makes clear in his two-volume study on the 1924 election, when at the helm, Coolidge took charge and it would become

---

[164] Coolidge, Have Faith in Massachusetts 46; Address at the home of Augustus P. Gardner, Hamilton, Massachusetts, September 1916.
[165] Calvin Coolidge, letter to Edward T. Clark, 21 October 1932, Edward T. Clark Papers, Manuscript Division, Library of Congress, Washington, D. C.

clear he led the country, the Party and the agenda.[166]

90. Taxation

"We can not finance the country, we can not improve social conditions, through any system of injustice, even if we attempt to inflict it upon the rich. Those who suffer the most harm will be the poor...The wise and correct course to follow in taxation and all other economic legislation is not to destroy those who have already secured success but to create conditions under which every one will have a better chance to be successful."[167]

"By reason of what I saw and heard in my early life, I came to have a good working knowledge of the practical side of government. I understood that it consisted of restraints which the people had imposed upon themselves in order to promote the

---

[166] Edward Ranson, The American Presidential Election of 1924: A Political Study of Calvin Coolidge, 2 vols. (Lewiston, NY: Edwin Mellon, 2008) 1:257ff.

[167] Coolidge, Foundations of the Republic 202; Inaugural Address, March 4, 1925.

common welfare. As I went about with my father when he collected taxes, I knew that when taxes were laid some one had to work to earn the money to pay them. I saw that a public debt was a burden on all the people in a community...["]168

91. Thrift

"I favor the policy of economy, not because I wish to save money, but because I wish to save people. The men and women of this country who toil are the ones who bear the cost of the Government. Every dollar that we carelessly waste means that their life will be so much the more meager. Every dollar that we prudently save means that their life will be so much the more abundant. Economy is idealism in its most practical form."169

168 Coolidge, Autobiography 27.
169 Coolidge, Foundations of the Republic 201;
Inaugural Address, March 4, 1925.

92. Time Management

"You talk back."[170] Coolidge's retort when asked by his successor, Governor Channing Cox, how he had enough time to get his work done with all the visitors every day.

93. Toleration

"Progress depends very largely on the encouragement of variety. Whatever tends to standardize the community, to establish fixed and rigid modes of thought, tends to fossilize society. If we all believed the same thing and thought the same thoughts and applied the same valuations to all the occurrences about us, we should reach a state of equilibrium closely akin to an intellectual and spiritual paralysis. It is the ferment of ideas, the clash of disagreeing judgments, the privilege of the individual to develop his own thoughts and shape his own character that makes progress possible...I make no plea for leniency toward those who are criminal or vicious, are open enemies of society and are not prepared to accept the

---

[170] Hannaford 168; Fuess 472.

true standards of our citizenship. By tolerance I do not mean indifference to evil. I mean respect for different kinds of good. Whether one traces his Americanisms back three centuries to the Mayflower, or three years to the steerage, is not half so important as whether his Americanism of to-day is real and genuine."[171]

94. Turnout

"What we need is organization work more than speech making."[172]

95. Using Technology

Senate majority leader, James Watson, remembers talking with Coolidge on the use of radio, "One day on the Mayflower [Presidential yacht], he said to me: 'I am very fortunate that I came in with the radio. I can't make an engaging, rousing, or

---

[171] Coolidge, Foundations of the Republic 296, 298; Speech before the American Legion Convention, Omaha, Nebraska, October 6, 1925.
[172] Calvin Coolidge, letter to Edward T. Clark, 21 September 1932, Manuscript Division, Library of Congress, Washington, D. C.

oratorical speech to a crowd as you can, and so all I can do is to stand up and talk to them in a matter-of-fact way about the issues of the campaign; but I have a good radio voice, and now I can get my messages across to them without acquainting them with my lack of oratorical ability or without making any rhetorical display in their presence.' He laughed about as heartily as I ever knew him to do over what he regarded as his singular good fortune in this respect. The truth about it is that everybody heard him with keen pleasure, because they felt that they were listening to an honest man who was giving them his sincere thoughts on the questions under discussion."[173]

96. Vice

"The problem of preventing vice and crime and of restraining personal and organized selfishness is as old as human experience. We shall not find for it an immediate and

---

[173] James Watson, As I Knew Them: Memoirs of James E. Watson, Former United States Senator from Indiana, (Indianapolis: Bobbs-Merrill Company, 1936) 239.

complete solution in an amendment to the Federal Constitution, an act of Congress, or in the findings of a new board or commission. There is no magic in government not possessed by the public at large, by which these things can be done. The people cannot divest themselves of their really great burdens by undertaking to provide that they shall hereafter be borne by the government."[174]

97. Victory and Defeat

"I called on many of the voters personally, sent out many letters, spoke at many ward rallies and kept my poise. In the end most of my old Democratic friends voted for me, and I won..."[175]

"Since we did not win the natural reaction will be to begin to blame each other for the defeat. That is no doubt going on but I have never once heard us suggestive of a criticism of your conduct of the campaign. I feel sure

---

[174] Coolidge, Price of Freedom 204-205; Address before the American Bar Association, August 10, 1922.
[175] Coolidge, Autobiography 100-101.

that you will find nothing but gratitude and praise for the work you did and the sacrifices you made. You will recall our victory with the aid of the dissatisfied in 1920 and how near it came to wrecking our party. You will see the same difficulty much enlarged after March 4 for our successor. I want you to know how grateful I am for your public service."[176]

98. Vision

Longtime friend of the Coolidges, Benjamin F. Felt, offers this analysis on Cal, "By some magic, never fully explained, this outwardly forbidding New Englander with unerring sense of direction cut his own trail to the hearthstone of millions of homes where his face had never been seen--except in pictures--or his voice heard--except by radio. There was about him the stuff that legends are made of, but he was not legendary. He was real. If there was magic, it was his magic. What was done to reveal him to the people

---

[176] Calvin Coolidge, letter to Everett Sanders, 25 November 1932, Everett Sanders Papers Manuscript Division, Library of Congress, Washington, D. C.

none did so effectively as he. It might well be said of him what he said of Lincoln: 'About him there was never any needless thing. No useless burdens held him back. No wilderness of tangled ideas bewildered his vision.' "[177]

"It has been the good fortune of our people that in times of crises they have had at the head of their government the man suited to the task beyond any other man then known to them. Calvin Coolidge is in that class of Presidents...No example from the White House would be impressive if made for the occasion only; it had to have the backing of lifelong habit. Coolidge gave it that backing. He did not suddenly acquire those traits; they are his by intuition. Neither great power nor the pressure to seek quick solutions of pending problems has ever led him from them. The people knew this of Coolidge...Coolidge believes that back of every advance there must be effort and purpose if the advance is to count, and he knows that effort and purpose require time.

---

[177] Benjamin F. Felt, "Some Points of View About Calvin Coolidge," Vermont History 23.4 (October 1955): 313.

He is willing to wait results, but waiting does not mean idly hoping; he is working to accomplish all the time."[178]

99. Voting

"When depression in business comes we begin to be very conservative in our financial affairs. We save our money and take no chances in its advancement. Yet in our political actions we go in the opposite direction. We begin to support radical measures and cast our votes for those who advance the most reckless proposals. This is a curious and illogical reaction. When times are good we might take a chance on a radical government. But when we are financially weakened we need the soundest and wisest of men and measures."[179]

"When we vote for anything but the best, we cheat ourselves, our families and our country."[180]

---

[178] Henry L. Stoddard, As I Knew Them: Presidents from Grant to Coolidge (New York: Harper and Brothers, 1927): 533-534.
[179] Lathem, Calvin Coolidge Says 154; Column from October 7, 1930.

"Persons who have the right to vote are trustees for the benefit of their country and their countrymen. They have no right to say they do not care. They must care. They have no right to say that whatever the result of the election they can get along. They must remember that their country and their countrymen cannot get along, cannot remain sound, cannot preserve its institutions, cannot protect its citizens, cannot maintain its place in the world, unless those who have the right to vote do sustain and do guide the course of public affairs by the thoughtful exercise of that right on election day."[181]

"With a careless, indifferent, uninformed electorate a republic will deteriorate into a very bad form of government. It will fall into the hands of the incompetent and the vicious. Good government under our system depends on the ballot box...We cannot receive what we do not give. Put good government into the ballot box."[182]

---

[180] Ibid 172; Column from October 28, 1930.
[181] Coolidge, Foundations of the Republic 178-179; Portion of a radio address broadcast from the White House, November 3, 1924.
[182] Lathem, Calvin Coolidge Says 170; Column from

100. Washington

"It is necessary to watch people in Washington all the time to keep them from unnecessary expenditure of money. They have lived off the national Government so long in that city that they are inclined to regard any sort of employment as a Christmas tree, and if we are not careful, they will run up a big expense bill on us."[183]

"I never knew so much meanness existed in the world as I listened to in Washington,...nearly every man who came was seeking something--either office or legislation he desired or defeated. Few came to urge measures or men for the public good--though nearly all professed it. I had had some experiences of that kind, of course, in other executive positions, but I was not prepared for so much of it and with so much persistent under-cover pressure. It seemed strange to me that a President, if he is to avoid mistakes, has to suspect and resist

---

October 25, 1930.

[183] Bernard Baruch, "His Silence and His Thrift," Good Housekeeping February 1935: 183.

almost every suggestion from callers until he can look into it most searchingly--and then usually ignore it. Some of my visitors, after leaving the White House, criticized me to others for my silence. If they had known my thoughts while I listened to them they would have praised me for not speaking."[184]

101. Work

"Work is not a curse, it is the prerogative of intelligence, the only means to manhood, and the measure of civilization. Savages do not work."[185]

---

[184] Henry L. Stoddard, It Costs To Be President (New York: Harper & Brothers, 1938) 125-126; Part of a conversation between Mr. Stoddard and Mr. Coolidge on the front porch of the Homestead.
[185] Coolidge, Have Faith in Massachusetts 13; Address given to the Amherst College Alumni Association, Boston, February 4, 1916.

TIMELINE

1 July 1872 – John Calvin Coolidge is born in Plymouth Notch, Vermont, to John and Victoria Coolidge.

November 1875 – On a visit to Montpelier, Grandfather Coolidge places 3 year old Calvin in the Governor's chair of the Vermont State House.

3 January 1879 – Grace Anna Goodhue is born in Burlington, Vermont, to Andrew and Lemira Goodhue.

14 March 1885 – Calvin's mother, Victoria, dies at age 39. Calvin is twelve.

8 September 1891 – Father John remarries – local schoolteacher Carrie Brown.

17 September 1891-26 June 1895 – Calvin completes education at Amherst College.

23 September 1895 – Calvin begins reading law at firm of Hammond and Field, Northampton, MA.

1 February 1898 – Calvin opens his own law office for practice in Northampton.

Autumn 1898 – Grace begins University of Vermont, graduates 1902.

6 December 1898 – Calvin elected councilman from Ward 2, Northampton.

18 January 1900 – Calvin elected city solicitor by Northampton's City Council.

17 January 1901 – Calvin reelected city solicitor.

4 June 1903 – Calvin appointed Clerk of Courts for Hampshire County, Massachusetts.

January 1904 – Calvin elected secretary, Northampton Republican Committee; chairman by spring.

Spring 1904, Calvin meets Grace.

4 October 1905 – Calvin and Grace married in Burlington, Vermont.

5 December 1905 – Calvin loses bid for School Board by 94 votes.

7 September 1906 – Birth of John, their first son.

6 November 1906 – Calvin elected to Massachusetts General Court as State Representative.

5 November 1907 – Calvin reelected to General Court.

13 April 1908 – Calvin Jr. is born.

7 December 1909 – Calvin elected Mayor of Northampton.

6 December 1910 – Calvin is reelected Mayor.

7 November 1911 – Calvin elected State Senator.

January 1912 – Calvin named chairman of important Agriculture, Legal Affairs, and Railroad Committees.

February 1912 – Calvin appointed chairman, special committee to settle Lawrence strike.

5 November 1912 – Calvin reelected State Senator.

1 January 1913 – Calvin named chairman of special committee on improved transportation in western Massachusetts.

12 June 1913 – Calvin sees bill for improved transportation pass over Governor's veto.

4 November 1913 – Calvin is reelected for third time as State Senator.

7 January 1914 – Calvin elected President of the Massachusetts Senate.

6 January 1915 – Calvin is reelected as President of the Massachusetts Senate.

2 November 1915 – Calvin elected Lt. Governor of Massachusetts.

7 November 1916 – Calvin reelected Lt. Governor.

6 November 1917 – Calvin again reelected Lt. Governor.

5 November 1918 – Calvin elected Governor of Massachusetts.

4 November 1919 – Calvin reelected Governor.

18 May 1920 Stepmother Carrie Brown Coolidge dies at age 63.

2 November 1920 – Calvin elected Vice President of the United States

4 March 1921 – Calving is inaugurated as Vice President, presides over United States Senate.

3 August 1923 – Calvin inaugurated in early morning hours as thirtieth President of the United States at family Homestead upon learning of death of President Harding.

6 December 1923 – Coolidge delivers First Annual Message outlining policies, first to be broadcast.

12 June 1924 – Calvin wins nomination for President on first ballot.

7 July 1924 – Calvin Jr. dies of septicemia at Walter Reed Hospital, Washington, D.C.

4 November 1924 – Calvin elected in his own right as President of the United States with 54 percent of total popular vote, 72% of total electoral vote.

4 March 1925 – Coolidge administered oath of office, first to deliver Inaugural Address via radio.

18 March 1926 – Coolidge's father, John, dies at home at age 81.

2 August 1927 – Calvin announces, "I do not choose to run for President in nineteen twenty-eight."

4 March 1929 – Calvin leaves Office; Succeeded by Herbert Hoover.

5 January 1933 – Calvin dies at home in Northampton, Massachusetts, age 60.

Sources

Andreasen, Joel J. "Calvin Coolidge: Puritan Progressive." MA

Thesis. University of Massachusetts, 2004.

Anthony, Carl Sferrazza. America's First Families: An Inside

View of 200 Years of PrivateLife in the White House. New

York: Touchstone Book, 2001.

Blair, John L., ed. "The Clark-Coolidge Correspondence

and the Election of 1932," Vermont History 34:2

(April 1966): 83-114.

Bryn-Jones, David. Frank B. Kellogg: A Biography. New

York: G. P. Putnam's Sons, 1937.

Calabresi, Steven G. and Christopher S. Yoo. The Unitary

Executive: Presidential Power from Washington to Bush.

New Haven: Yale University Press, 2008.

Campaign Speeches of 1932 by President Hoover and Ex-

President Coolidge. Garden City, NY: Doubleday, Doran &

Company, 1933.

Cannadine, David. Mellon: An American Life. New York:

Alfred A. Knopf, 2006.

Clark, Edward T. Papers. Box 3, Folders 1-6, Manuscript

135

Division, Library of Congress, Washington, D.C.

Coolidge, Calvin. Have Faith in Massachusetts: A Collection of Speeches and Messages. Boston: Houghton Mifflin

Company, 1919.

---. The Price of Freedom: Speeches and Addresses. New York: Charles Scribner's Sons, 1924.

---. Foundations of the Republic: Speeches and Addresses. New York: Charles Scribner's Sons, 1926.

---. The Autobiography. New York: Cosmopolitan Book Corporation, 1929.

---. "The Republican Case," The Saturday Evening Post September 10, 1932.

Coolidge, Grace. Grace Coolidge: An Autobiography. Eds. Lawrence E. Wikander and Robert H. Ferrell. Worland, WY: High Plains, 1992.

---. "The Real Calvin Coolidge," Good Housekeeping February 1935: 18-21, 181-191.

---. "The Real Calvin Coolidge," Good Housekeeping March 1935: 22-25, 214-227.

---. "The Real Calvin Coolidge," Good Housekeeping April

1935: 38-41, 197-208.

---. "The Real Calvin Coolidge," <u>Good Housekeeping</u> May 1935:

38-39, 247-259.

---. "The Real Calvin Coolidge," <u>Good Housekeeping</u> June

1935: 42-43, 198-210.

"Coolidge Loaned Money to His Hotel-Room Thief." <u>The</u>

<u>Dispatch</u> 6 August 1983

<https://news.google.com/newspapers?nid=1734&dat

=19830806&id=64EcAAAAIBAJ&sjid=fiIEAAAAIBAJ&

pg=5743,3927086&hl=en>.

Cornwell Jr., Elmer E. <u>Presidential Leadership of Public</u>

<u>Opinion</u>. Westport, CT: Greenwood, 1965.

Danelski, David J. and Joseph S. Tulchin, eds. <u>The</u>

<u>Autobiographical Notes of Charles Evans Hughes</u>.

Cambridge: Harvard University Press, 1973.

Dawes, Charles G. <u>Notes as Vice President 1928-1929</u>. Boston:

Little, Brown, and Company, 1935.

Dean, Charles J. "Mayor Coolidge," <u>Vermont History</u> 24:4

(October 1956): 327-330.

Felt, Benjamin F. "Some Points of View About Calvin

Coolidge," <u>Vermont History</u> 23:4 (October 1955): 312-317.

Fuess, Claude M. <u>Calvin Coolidge: The Man From Vermont</u>.

 Boston: Little, Brown, and Company, 1940.

Gerhardt, Michael J. <u>The Forgotten Presidents: Their Untold</u>

<u>Constitutional Legacy</u>. New York: Oxford University Press,

 2013.

Green, Horace. <u>The Life of Calvin Coolidge</u>. New York:

 Duffield & Company, 1924.

Griffin, Solomon Bulkley. <u>W. Murray Crane: A Man and</u>

<u>Brother</u>. Boston: Little, Brown, and Company, 1926.

Hannaford, Peter, ed. <u>The Quotable Calvin Coolidge: Sensible</u>

<u>Words for a New Century</u>. Bennington, VT: Images from

 the Past, 2001.

Hathorn, Guy B. "The Political Career of C. Bascom Slemp."

 Diss. Duke, 1950.

Haynes, John Earl, ed. <u>Calvin Coolidge and the Coolidge Era:</u>

<u>Essays on the History of the 1920s</u>. Washington, D. C.:

 Library of Congress, 1998.

Hennessy, Michael E. <u>Calvin Coolidge: From A Green</u>

<u>Mountain Farm to the White House</u>. New York: G. P.

Putnam's Sons, 1924.

Howland, Hewitt H. <u>Dwight Whitney Morrow: A Sketch in</u>

<u>Admiration</u>. New York: Century Company, 1930.

Johnson, Carolyn W. <u>Winthrop Murray Crane: A Study in</u>

<u>Republican Leadership 1892-1920</u>. Northampton, MA:

    Smith College, 1967.

Johnson, Charles C. <u>Why Coolidge Matters: Leadership</u>

<u>Lessons from America's Most Underrated President</u>. New

    York: Encounter Books, 2013.

Johnson, Paul. "The Last Arcadia," <u>Modern Times: The World</u>

<u>from the Twenties to the Nineties</u>. Rev. ed. New York:

    HarperCollins, 1991.

Krug, Larry L. <u>The 1924 Coolidge-Dawes Lincoln Tour</u>. Atlgen,

    PA: Schiffer, 2007.

Lathem, Edward C., ed. <u>Calvin Coolidge Says: Over three</u>

<u>hundred dispatches prepared by former-President</u>

<u>Coolidge and syndicated to newspapers in the United</u>

<u>States and abroad during 1930-1931</u>. Plymouth: Calvin

    Coolidge Memorial Foundation, 1972.

---, ed. <u>Meet Calvin Coolidge: The Man Behind the Myth</u>.

Brattleboro, Stephen Greene Press, 1960.

---, ed. <u>Your Son, Calvin Coolidge: A Selection of Letters from Calvin Coolidge to his Father</u>. Montpelier: Vermont

    Historical Society, 1968.

Long, Henry F., comp. <u>Public Record of Calvin Coolidge</u>. Ms.

    Coll. 19. State Library of Massachusetts, Boston.

McKee, John Hiram. <u>Coolidge Wit and Wisdom: 125 Short Stories About "Cal</u>." New York: Frederick A. Stokes, 1933.

Murray, Robert K. <u>The Harding Era: Warren G. Harding and His Administration</u>. Newtown, CT: American Political

    Biography, 1969.

National Notary Association. <u>Why Coolidge Matters: How Civility in Politics Can Bring a Nation Together</u>.

    Chatsworth, CA: NNA, 2010.

Pietrusza, David. <u>1920: The Year of the Six Presidents</u>. New

    York: Carroll & Graf Publishers, 2007.

---, ed. <u>Calvin Coolidge: A Documentary Biography</u>. Church &

    Reid Books, 2013.

---, ed. <u>Silent Cal's Almanack: The Homespun Wit and Wisdom of Vermont's Calvin Coolidge</u>. A Createspace

Book, 2008.

Quint, Howard, and Robert Ferrell, eds. <u>The Talkative</u>
<u>President: The Off-the Record Press Conferences of Calvin</u>
<u>Coolidge</u>. Amherst: University of Massachusetts, 1964.

Randolph, Mary. <u>Presidents and First Ladies</u>. New York: D-
 Appleton-Century Company, 1936.

Ranson, Edward. <u>The American Presidential Election of 1924:</u>
<u>A Political Study of Calvin Coolidge</u>. 2 vols. Lewiston, NY:
 Edwin Mellon, 2008.

Richardson, James D., ed. <u>Supplement to the Messages and</u>
<u>Papers of the Presidents</u>. New York: Bureau of National
 Literature, 1929.

Rogers, Cameron. <u>The Legend of Calvin Coolidge</u>. Garden
 City, NY: Doubleday, Doran & Company, 1928.

Rugg, Arthur Prentice. <u>Calvin Coolidge Memorial Address</u>
<u>Delivered before the Joint Meetings of the Two Houses of</u>
<u>Congress as a Tribute of Respect to the Late President of</u>
<u>the United States</u>. US 72nd Cong., 2nd sess. Senate Doc.
 186. Washington: GPO, 1933.

Sanders, Everett. Papers. Box 1, Folder 1, Manuscript Division,

Library of Congress, Washington, D.C.

Sawyer, Roland D. Cal Coolidge, President. Boston: Four Seas

Company, 1924.

Shlaes, Amity. Coolidge. New York: HarperCollins, 2013.

Silver, Thomas B. Coolidge and the Historians. Durham:

Carolina Academic, 1982.

Slemp, C. Bascom, ed. The Mind of the President: As Revealed

by Himself in His Own Words. Garden City, NY:

Doubleday, Page & Company, 1926.

Slemp, C. Bascom, Papers, 1866-1944, Accession #9507,

Special Collections Dept., University of Virginia Library,

Charlottesville, VA.

Sobel, Robert. Coolidge: An American Enigma. Washington,

D. C.: Regnery, 1998.

Starling, Edmund. Starling of the White House. Chicago:

People's Book Club, 1916.

Stern, Sheldon, ed. "Calvin Coolidge: Examining the Evidence:

A Conference at the John F. Kennedy Library, July 30-31,

1998," The New England Journal of History 55:1 (Fall 1998),

1-122.

142

---. "The Struggle to Teach the Whole Story: Calvin Coolidge

and American History Education," The New England

Journal of History 53:2 (Fall 1996), 38-52.

Stoddard, Henry L. As I Knew Them: Presidents and Politics

from Grant to Coolidge. New York: Harper and Brothers,

1927.

---. It Costs To Be President. New York: Harper & Brothers,

1938.

Thompson, Charles Willis. Presidents I've Known and Two

Near Presidents. Indianapolis: Bobbs-Merrill Company,

1929.

Thompson, Robert J. Adequate Brevity: A Collation and Co-

ordination of the Mental Processes and Reactions of Calvin

Coolidge, as Expressed in his Addresses and Messages, and

Constituting a Self-Delineation of his Character and Ideals.

Chicago: M. A. Donohue & Company, 1924.

Tucker III, Garland S. The High Tide of American

Conservatism: Davis, Coolidge, and the 1924 Election.

Austin: Emerald Book Company, 2010.

Wallace, Jerry L. Calvin Coolidge: Our First Radio President.

Plymouth: Five Corners, 2008.

Washburn, R. M. <u>Calvin Coolidge: His First Biography – From</u>
<u>Cornerstone to Capstone to the Accession</u>. Boston: Small,

Maynard and Company, 1923.

Watson, James. <u>As I Knew Them: Memoirs of James E.</u>
<u>Watson, Former United States Senator from Indiana</u>.

Indianapolis: Bobbs-Merrill Company, 1936.

White, William Allen. <u>Calvin Coolidge: The Man Who Is</u>
<u>President</u>. New York: Macmillan Company, 1925.

Whiting, Edward Elwell. <u>Calvin Coolidge: A Contemporary</u>
<u>Estimate</u>. Boston: The Atlantic Monthly, 1923.

---. <u>Calvin Coolidge: His Ideals of Citizenship as Revealed</u>
<u>through Speeches and Writings</u>. Boston: W. A. Wilde

Company, 1924.

Woods, Robert A. <u>The Preparation of Calvin Coolidge</u>.

Cambridge: Riverside, 1924.